Emotional Mastery Unleased

Dr M.k.Brown

Published by Dr M.k.Brown, 2024.

While every precaution has been taken in the preparation of this book, the publisher assumes no responsibility for errors or omissions, or for damages resulting from the use of the information contained herein.

EMOTIONAL MASTERY UNLEASED

First edition. January 27, 2024.

ISBN: 979-8224759989

Written by Dr M.k.Brown.

Table of Contents

Emotional Mastery Unleashed

Emotional Intelligence for Everyday Triumphs, Strategies for Thriving in Work, Relationships, and Self-Discovery

Introduction

There's a profound domain waiting to be explored, one that holds the key to unlocking the whole range of human experience, in a world that frequently runs at an unrelenting pace, where the cacophony of daily existence drowns the whispers of our inner selves. Greetings and welcome to "Emotional Mastery Unleashed," a guide that calls you to take an immersive journey into the depths of emotional intelligence. It invites you to actively engage in the symphony of your own emotions rather than just witnessing it.

In the pages that follow, we set out on an extraordinary trip exploring the subtleties of emotional intelligence as a means of achieving personal fulfillment, deepening relationships, and cultivating a strong sense of self. Here, emotional intelligence is more than just a theory; it's a dynamic, breathing force that enables you to negotiate the intricacies of your inner world, speak the language of your heart, and create a life that fulfills and is authentic.

We work with a large and complex canvas that is colored with the shades of resilience, empathy, self-awareness, and the nuanced interaction of emotions. Every chapter reveals the elements that make up the fundamental structure of emotional intelligence, acting as a brushstroke. The book is a road map that will help you navigate the complexities of relationships and recognize the dance of emotions within. It will also provide you with practical advice and wisdom on how to improve personally.

This is not a book that only presents abstract ideas. Rather, it serves as a walking companion with you, providing useful advice and practical activities that help close the knowledge gap between comprehension and implementation. You will engage in reflective practices, examine real-world situations, and discover the skills that help you turn emotional intelligence into concrete actions as you progress through the chapters.

The dedication to a holistic strategy for personal development—one that recognizes the interdependence of the mind, heart, and spirit—lays the foundation of these pages. The techniques and perspectives offered here go far beyond the spheres of professional success or outward accomplishments; they penetrate deep into your being, promoting resilience, enhancing connections, and cultivating a sense of purpose that is in line with who you truly are.

Think of this book as a blueprint, and yourself as the designer of your emotional terrain. You are encouraged to consider, delve into, and mold your own story as you interact with the material. The book aims to empower you to ask the proper questions and find the answers that are in line with your particular journey rather than offering pre-made solutions.

I therefore extend an invitation to you to turn the page and go on a life-changing adventure with an open heart and an inquiring mind. This book serves as a compass, pointing the way toward emotional mastery, fulfilling relationships, and reaching your maximum potential, regardless of whether you're on the verge of self-discovery or want to learn more about emotional intelligence.

I trust that this journey will bring profound insights, resilient growth, and a life painted with vibrant hues of emotional intelligence. Step into the world of Emotional Mastery where the journey towards self-awareness becomes the gateway to a life filled with authenticity, richness, and prosperity.

Chapter 1: Understanding Emotional Intelligence

1.1 Exploring the Components of Emotional Intelligence

Emotions are the colorful threads in the complex fabric of the human experience that weave together our everyday lives, influencing our relationships, behaviors, and thoughts. Emotional intelligence is the ability to recognize these feelings and use them to one's advantage. It is a concept that goes beyond psychological theory and is now considered essential to both personal and professional success. As we set out on this path, a thorough examination of the essential components of emotional intelligence is our first stop.

Emotional Intelligence

Emotional intelligence, sometimes shortened to EQ (Emotional Quotient) or EI, is the capacity to identify, comprehend, control, and make efficient use of one's own emotions in addition to navigating and influencing those of others.

Emotional intelligence, which was first defined by psychologists Peter Salovey and John D. Mayer, made popular by novelist and science journalist Daniel Goleman, goes beyond conventional intelligence tests to highlight the vital role emotions play in our success and general well-being.

The Four Emotional Intelligence Components

1. Awareness of Oneself: The Basis of Emotional Intelligence

Self-awareness, or the capacity to identify and comprehend one's own emotions in the moment, is the fundamental component of emotional intelligence. This is being aware of the subtleties of emotions, accurately identifying them, and comprehending how they affect attitudes and actions. People who are very self-aware have a profound awareness of their motives, values, and areas of strength and weakness. We explore useful methods for developing this fundamental ability in this book, such as journaling, mindfulness exercises, and introspective practices.

1. Autoregulation: Handling the Harmonious Emotions

Self-regulation is the skill of successfully managing and controlling one's emotions, whereas self-awareness establishes the foundation. It entails negotiating the turbulent ocean of emotions without becoming overwhelmed and reacting to circumstances with consideration as opposed to haste. Chapter 3 provides readers with a toolkit to develop emotional stability and control, ranging from stress management methods to resilience-building tactics.

1. **Social Awareness: Managing Others' Emotional Environment**

Being acutely aware of the emotions of those around us is a component of emotional intelligence that goes beyond self-awareness. Recognizing and comprehending the emotions of others, deciphering nonverbal clues, and exhibiting empathy are all components of social awareness. People with high social awareness build genuine connections and skillfully negotiate social dynamics through effective communication, attentive listening, and enhanced observational abilities.

1. **Emotional Harmony in Relationship Management: An Art**

The capacity to properly navigate relationships is the ultimate test of emotional intelligence. Building and sustaining healthy connections through emotional awareness and regulation is the goal of relationship management. The main focus of Chapter 5 is on relationship-building, communication, and conflict resolution practices that give readers the tools they need to create happy, healthy relationships in both their personal and professional lives.

Even if each of these elements is discussed separately, it's important to understand how they are related. While social awareness guides relationship management, self-awareness establishes the groundwork for self-regulation. An emotional intelligence that is comprehensive and well-rounded is the outcome of these elements working together harmoniously.

1.2 The Science Behind Emotional Intelligence

The concept of emotional intelligence (EI) is a tribute to the significant interplay between our emotions and cognitive processes in the complex tapestry of human psychology. As we dive deep, it is essential to examine the scientific foundations that support and give light on the importance of emotional intelligence.

The Emotional Intelligence Research Pioneers

Peter Salovey and John D. Mayer, two psychologists, made significant contributions to the field of emotional intelligence research in the early 1990s. Their groundbreaking study established the groundwork for the formal definition of emotional intelligence and put out a paradigm that focused on the capacity to recognize, comprehend, regulate, and utilize emotions. With the publication of his best-selling book "Emotional Intelligence" in 1995, famous science writer and journalist Daniel Goleman introduced the idea to the general public.

Emotional Intelligence's Multifaceted Nature

According to science, emotional intelligence is a constellation of skills and abilities that work together rather than a single characteristic. Emotional and cognitive processes are integrated as the fundamental component of emotional intelligence. An important function for the limbic system, including the prefrontal cortex and amygdala, is played in this complex dance between emotion and logic. The prefrontal cortex, which is in charge of executive functions, modifies and controls these emotional responses, whereas the amygdala, sometimes known as the emotional center of the brain, interprets emotional stimuli and triggers quick reactions.

Neuroplasticity: The Adaptive Capability of the Brain

The notion of neuroplasticity, or the brain's capacity to rearrange itself and create new neural connections throughout life, is one of the most intriguing parts of the science underlying emotional intelligence. The brain's malleability and ability to change in response to events, instruction, and deliberate effort are highlighted by neuroplasticity. People who participate in emotional intelligence-boosting activities, such mindfulness exercises and cognitive restructuring, cause favorable alterations in the brain circuitry linked to emotional control and self-awareness.

Prefrontal Cortex and Emotion Regulation

In the field of emotional intelligence science, the prefrontal cortex comes to light as a major participant, especially when it comes to emotion regulation. Higher-order cognitive processes including impulse control, emotional management, and decision-making are controlled by this area of the brain. Prefrontal brain activity has been shown to rise with emotional intelligence, suggesting that people are better able to control and regulate their emotions.

The Mirror Neuron's Function in Empathy

Mirror neuron activity and empathy, a critical aspect of emotional intelligence, are closely related. These neurons are dispersed throughout the brain and fire when someone performs an action or watches someone else execute the same action. The brain underpinnings of empathy are formed by this mirroring mechanism, which enables people to comprehend and relate to the feelings of others. The function of mirror neurons provides light on the neurological basis of our capacity for emotional communication with others, as we delve deeper into the science of emotional intelligence.

The Hormonal Orchestra: Emotional States, Oxytocin, and Cortisol

Hormonal science is part of the science of emotional intelligence, going beyond cerebral circuitry. Known as the stress hormone, cortisol is closely linked to emotional states and is essential to the body's fight-or-flight reaction. Conversely, oxytocin, which is also referred to as the "love hormone" or the "bonding hormone," is linked to good emotional experiences, social connection, and trust. Gaining knowledge of the intricate interactions between these hormones can help explain the physiological foundations of emotional intelligence.

Emotional Intelligence: The Impact of Environment and Genetics

The interaction of genetics and environmental influences must be acknowledged, even if the science of emotional intelligence stresses the neurological and hormonal components. According to research, there may be a genetic component to emotional intelligence, meaning that a person's inclination toward particular emotional competences may be influenced by genetic variances. Environmental factors that shape and hone emotional intelligence throughout a person's life include early experiences and social interactions.

Implications and Uses of Emotional Intelligence Research in Practice

It is becoming clear that emotional intelligence is more than simply an abstract idea—rather, it is a real, concrete feature of human psychology with broad implications—as the science underlying it being unlocked. Research on emotional intelligence has many real-world implications, from organizational management and mental health to education and leadership development. By being aware of the neurological and physiological underpinnings, people can adopt a scientific perspective when developing emotional intelligence, which promotes deliberate and focused development.

Acquiring information about the science of emotional intelligence is more than simply a cerebral endeavor; it's a call to unleash one's inner potential by bridging the gap between emotion and reason.

1.3 Assessing Your Current EI Level

When we explore the vast field of emotional intelligence, we get to a turning point where we have to look inward. Finding out your current Emotional Intelligence (EI) score is the first step in a contemplative journey that will help you grow, become more self-aware, and achieve emotional mastery.

Comprehending the Importance of Self-Evaluation

It's important to understand why assessing one's own emotional intelligence is a critical first step in the process of personal development before diving into the practical components of self-assessment. As a compass, emotional intelligence helps people navigate the complex world of emotions, relationships, and decision-making. You can learn a lot about the subtleties of your emotional landscape, your areas of strength and progress, and your present emotional intelligence (EI) by taking an assessment.

Self-evaluation is an act of self-compassion rather than judgment; it's a chance to gain a deeper understanding of oneself and develop the empowerment to deal with the challenges of life gracefully and resiliently. The assessment procedure is a flexible instrument that can be tailored to each person's particular traits and experiences rather than a strict examination.

Evaluation Components: A Comprehensive Examination

An in-depth analysis of the fundamental elements that make up emotional intelligence is required to determine your present emotional intelligence level. The evaluation procedure is complex, including a range of factors to provide a complete picture of your emotional terrain.

1. **Introspection as a Mirror of Self-Awareness**

The foundation of emotional intelligence, self-awareness, asks you to look in the mirror and honestly assess your emotional experiences. You will take a voyage of self-discovery with reflection exercises, journaling prompts, and mindful contemplation. A baseline for determining your current state of self-awareness can be obtained by rating your capacity to identify and categorize your emotions in a variety of contexts.

1. **Controlling Your Emotions: Handling the Emotional Waves**

The self-regulation assessment explores your ability to control and regulate your emotional reactions. This assessment component asks you to investigate how well you navigate the ship of your emotions in the turbulent waters of life, from stress management techniques to assessing your resilience in the face of difficulties.

1. **Social Awareness: Perceiving the Feelings of Others**

Beyond inward reflection, emotional intelligence includes a keen understanding of the feelings of those around you. You'll evaluate your capacity to recognize emotional indicators and fully comprehend the feelings of others through scenarios, interactive exercises, and empathy tests. These skills are crucial for managing interpersonal interactions.

1. Managing Relationships: Creating Harmonious Emotions

The assessment's last dimension focuses on how skillfully you can handle relationships. This component provides insight into your ability to use emotional intelligence to establish meaningful connections and resolve interpersonal issues, through everything from conflict resolution scenarios to an evaluation of your communication skills.

Moving Through the Evaluation Process: A Directed Investigation

The evaluation procedure is a guided investigation rather than a solo project. Thought-provoking questions, realistic scenarios, and useful exercises provide readers with a road map for intentionally navigating their emotional environment. An overview, advice, and anecdotes are provided for every evaluation component, providing a framework for comprehending and analyzing the findings.

The evaluation is a dynamic tool designed to change with you, not a fixed snapshot. You might find trends, areas of strength, and opportunities for improvement as you work through the exercises. It's a call to honesty, acknowledging that the path to emotional mastery is an ongoing process of improvement and development.

A Growth Blueprint: Interpreting the Results

After the evaluation is finished, the following stage is to interpret the findings as a guide for improvement rather than as a judgment.

It offers a framework for interpreting your results, appreciating your accomplishments, and pinpointing areas in which deliberate improvement can result in profound transformation.

For example, having high self-awareness ratings indicates a solid foundation. Building on this, you can direct your attention toward improving other elements, including social awareness or relationship management. On the other hand, if self-regulation proves to be difficult for you, the book provides specific techniques and activities to improve this component of your emotional intelligence.

Participation in the Path to Emotional Proficiency

The evaluation procedure is assiduously integrated into the book's overall story, mingling with later chapters that offer focused techniques and activities to improve particular facets of emotional intelligence. It turns into more than just a stand-alone task; rather, it becomes a crucial part of your continuing story about achieving emotional mastery.

1.4 Importance of Emotional Intelligence in Personal Growth

In the field of personal development, emotional intelligence (EI) is a lighthouse that illuminates the way to self-awareness, empathy, and successful communication. It goes beyond simple intelligence and is essential in guiding one's path to total growth. Its significance is felt in many areas of life, including relationships, career achievement, and mental health.

Fundamentally, emotional intelligence (EI) is the capacity to understand and control emotions, both in oneself and in others. The foundation of emotional intelligence (EI) is self-awareness, which is the ability to acknowledge one's feelings, abilities, and how they affect behavior. This capacity for introspection serves as the cornerstone for personal development. People who are aware of their emotional terrain are better able to make decisions and resolve conflicts because they can see how emotions affect behavior.

Furthermore, empathy is a vital quality that develops stronger relationships with people and is fostered by having a high degree of emotional intelligence. People with empathy are able to put themselves in other people's shoes, comprehend their viewpoints, and react delicately. This ability to empathize not only strengthens interpersonal bonds but also fosters cooperation, teamwork, and successful leadership in a variety of contexts.

When it comes to personal development, EI fosters resilience and self-control. One of the characteristics of emotional intelligence is the capacity to control emotions, particularly under trying circumstances. Those who are skilled at it can handle tension, failures, and confrontations with poise and elegance. Rather of letting their emotions get in the way, they use them to their advantage by being composed and focused while overcoming obstacles in their way.

EI has a significant impact on verbal and nonverbal communication. People with higher emotional intelligence are better able to communicate their ideas and emotions, which promotes rapport and understanding. Effective and compassionate communication promotes trust and collaboration in both personal and professional contexts, which drives growth and achievement.

The workplace is evidence of the importance of emotional intelligence (EI) in human development. Employers want people with emotional intelligence in addition to technical talents in today's dynamic and connected environment. Emotionally intelligent leaders inspire and encourage their teams, guiding them toward shared objectives while fostering personal development. Additionally, emotional intelligence (EI) improves conflict resolution skills, reducing miscommunication and creating a peaceful workplace that promotes productivity.

Additionally, developing emotional intelligence has a substantial positive impact on mental health and wellbeing. People who have higher emotional intelligence also often have lower stress and anxiety levels. Through good recognition and regulation of their emotions, individuals develop resilience and mental toughness, therefore preserving their general welfare. Consequently, this establishes the foundation for ongoing personal development and satisfaction.

It takes time to become emotionally intelligent, however. It calls for commitment, introspection, and a readiness to accept vulnerability. To improve one's emotional intelligence, try writing, practicing mindfulness, and asking for feedback. Emotional intelligence may also be increased by partaking in activities that promote empathy, such as volunteering or paying attention to the experiences of others.

In summary, it is impossible to overestimate the role that emotional intelligence plays in human development. It acts as a compass, pointing people in the direction of better relationships, self-discovery, career success, and mental health. Through developing the abilities of self-awareness, empathy, self-control, and effective communication, people set themselves up for a rewarding path of ongoing self-improvement and overall development. A deeper awareness of who we are and the world around us becomes possible when we recognize and develop our emotional intelligence, which leads to a life that is more meaningful and fulfilling.

1.5 Benefits of Developing High Emotional Intelligence

Numerous benefits exist for those who comprehend and develop high emotional intelligence (EI) in the social, professional, and personal spheres. Empathy, which is often defined as the capacity to identify, comprehend, and regulate feelings in both oneself and other people, has a big impact on a lot of different aspects of life. Gaining strong emotional intelligence has the following significant advantages:

1. **Improved Connections**

Higher EI promotes stronger interpersonal relationships. People who are good at identifying emotions, both their own and others', are better able to handle social situations. Their ability to speak more effectively, show empathy, and decipher nonverbal clues results in deeper and more satisfying relationships.

1. **Enhanced Interaction**

Emotional intelligence facilitates successful dialogue. Individuals with high emotional intelligence (EI) can express their emotions and ideas clearly, preventing misunderstandings. They also listen well, understanding not only what is said but also the feelings that are hidden, which leads to deeper conversations.

1. **Reduction of Stress**

High EI people are better at handling stress. They are more adept at identifying stressors, controlling their emotions, and using coping strategies. This resilience helps in preserving mental health even under trying circumstances.

1. Resolving Conflicts

Empathy makes it easier to settle disputes peacefully. People are able to see things from several angles, maintain composure under pressure, and come up with win-win solutions. The capacity to resolve disputes amicably is very useful in both personal and professional contexts.

1. Skills in Leadership

High emotional intelligence is a common trait of exceptional leaders. They grasp team dynamics, excite and inspire others, and modify their leadership approach to fit the needs of various personalities. Cohesion between the team and a healthy work environment are fostered by EI leaders.

1. Making Decisions

A. higher level of emotional intelligence facilitates better decision-making. High EI people are able to strike a balance between emotion and reason, taking into account both intuitive insights and logical facts. Taking a balanced approach often results in more sensible and well considered conclusions.

2. More Compassion

Empathy, the foundation of emotional intelligence, enables people to comprehend the feelings and viewpoints of others. This skill develops stronger bonds, improves collaboration, and advances a society that is more accepting and understanding.

1. Switching

People with high EI are more flexible. They are better at adjusting to change and welcoming new circumstances with optimism. This capacity to adapt is essential in the fast-paced world of today because it enables people to flourish in a variety of settings.

1. Increased Self-Awareness

A. person with emotional intelligence is more self-aware. People with high emotional intelligence (EI) are more aware of their objectives, values, and areas of strength and weakness. Their ability to recognize themselves allows them to make decisions that are true to who they really are.

2. Weller-Being Partnerships

Relationships are often healthier for those with high EI, both personally and professionally. They establish a climate of mutual respect, trust, and open communication, which strengthens bonds and promotes general wellbeing.

1. Success in Career

Success in the workplace is increasingly linked to emotional intelligence (EI). People with high emotional intelligence (EI) are good at leadership, collaboration, and customer service. They often exhibit increased flexibility, resilience, and excellent stress management, all of which advance their careers.

1. Enhanced Mental Well-Being

Gaining emotional intelligence has a beneficial effect on mental health. People may live more balanced and happy lives by reducing anxiety, depression, and other mental health difficulties via improved understanding and management of emotions.

To sum up, developing strong emotional intelligence is not only advantageous but also necessary for one's own development, that of others, one's career, and one's general well-being. It enables people to make meaningful contributions to both their own and those around them by empowering them to manage the difficulties of life with resilience, empathy, and clarity.

Chapter 2: Cultivating Self-Awareness

2.1 Techniques for Recognizing Emotions

The first step toward developing emotional intelligence is realizing and comprehending emotions. This point explores many methods that people can use to become more adept at recognizing and understanding emotions in others as well as in themselves.

- **Introspection:** Start by focusing inside and becoming acutely aware of your own emotional emotions. This entails being aware of your emotions in various contexts. Frequent self-reflection helps identify trends and stressors, offering insightful information about your emotional terrain.

- **Awareness of Body Language:** A common way that emotions show up physically is through body language. You can tell what emotions someone is feeling by learning to analyze non-verbal clues including posture, gestures, and facial expressions. This ability is essential for both understanding other people and discovering your own hidden feelings.

• Using Active Listening Pay attention to the emotional content of the words as well as the spoken ones when you are conversing. Pay attention to the speaker's tone, pitch, and word choice. This improves your relationship with others and helps you comprehend the feelings that are conveyed through speech.

• **Practice Empathy:** Consider yourself from other people's perspectives. Try to put yourself in the shoes of others when you're in a particular circumstance.

Empathy, a crucial aspect of emotional intelligence, is developed in this way. In order to build deep connections and settle disputes, it is essential to be able to relate to and comprehend the sentiments of others.

• **Mindfulness Meditation:** Practice meditation to develop mindfulness. By practicing mindfulness, you can more deeply comprehend your inner world by learning to examine your thoughts and feelings without passing judgment.

Regular mindfulness meditation practice can help you become more conscious of your emotional reactions.

• **Developing Emotional Vocabulary:** In order to appropriately identify and communicate your emotions, broaden your emotional lexicon. The more accurate you are at recognizing your feelings, the more capable you are at handling them. This ability comes in especially handy when asking for help or discussing your feelings with others.

• **Journaling:** Make it a practice to keep a record of your feelings. This includes keeping a journal of your everyday activities and writing the feelings you have connected to different situations. This can eventually highlight recurrent emotional patterns, which can help pinpoint triggers and opportunities for personal development.

• **Technology Use:** Make use of tools and applications made to monitor and assess emotions. Certain applications employ artificial intelligence algorithms to evaluate your emotional condition by analyzing your facial expressions or language usage. These resources can offer insightful analysis and insightful criticism, serving as additional tools to support you on your path to emotional intelligence.

By applying these methods in your day-to-day activities, you establish a solid basis for identifying and comprehending feelings. Emotional intelligence is a multifaceted skill set that starts with the capacity to recognize and manage emotions. It also helps you become more self-aware. You'll become more adept at managing the complexity of both your own emotions and those of those around you as you get better at mastering these tactics.

2.2 Practices for Understanding Personal Triggers and Patterns

This part delves deeper into the concept of self-awareness and focuses on techniques that help recognize and comprehend personal patterns and triggers. Gaining emotional intelligence requires understanding what makes others feel a certain way and identifying patterns of behavior.

- **Contemplation of Past Events:** Spend some time thinking back on previous encounters that had a profound emotional effect. Think about both good and bad things that happen. It is possible to identify patterns and triggers that may be affecting your present emotional reactions by analyzing the feelings associated with these experiences.

- **Therapeutic Support:** Seek expert advice in therapy or counseling to better understand your emotional causes. A therapist can offer a secure setting for discussing past experiences, dispelling myths, and identifying patterns that might be causing present emotional outbursts.

- **Meditation Techniques:** Expand your mindfulness exercises to target your triggers in particular. When strong feelings arise, take a moment to notice them without acting on them right away. You can separate yourself from the emotion and get insight into its nature and source when you practice mindfulness.

0 **Maintain an Emotional Diary:** Keep a specific notebook for recording your feelings, particularly in trying times. Take note of the situation, your feelings, and your next steps.

This written documentation aids in the identification of recurrent patterns and triggers, enabling a more impartial study.

• **Ask Reliable People for Their Opinions:** Relatives, coworkers, or trusted pals can provide insightful analysis of your emotional tendencies. Invite frank and helpful criticism regarding how they see your responses to different circumstances. Observations from the outside can reveal information that is sometimes hard to notice internally.

0 Identify the Sensations in Your Body:** Certain bodily sensations frequently accompany emotional reactions. Be mindful of any physical responses, such as tightness in the muscles, an accelerated heartbeat, or nausea. These bodily signs may function as markers for underlying emotional stimuli.

• **Examine Influences During Childhood:** Emotional reactions in maturity are shaped by experiences during childhood. Examine early connections and experiences to learn the origins of some emotional triggers. Understanding these sources is essential to ending unhealthy habits and promoting emotional development.

• **Link Emotions to Fundamental Principles:** Consider how your feelings relate to your basic beliefs and how they differ from them. Your conduct may be influenced by specific triggers if your reactions don't align with your ideals. Authenticity and emotional stability are fostered when one's behaviors are consistent with one's principles.

• **Support or Group Configurations:** Engage in social settings where people have similar aspirations for self-discovery. Gaining knowledge and understanding from others going through comparable struggles might help you see personal triggers and patterns from a wider angle.

• **Consistent Visits:** Plan frequent self-evaluations to gauge your emotional health. By taking a proactive stance, you can recognize triggers before they intensify into strong emotional reactions. Relentless self-awareness cultivates a more deliberate and in control handling of emotions.

A combination of self-reflection, outside criticism, and a dedication to continuous self-discovery are necessary to comprehend personal triggers and patterns. By practicing these techniques, you can better understand the causes of your emotional reactions and develop the emotional intelligence necessary to handle difficult circumstances. The foundation for the later development of efficient self-regulation and general emotional mastery is laid by this increased awareness.

2.3 Journaling and Reflection Exercises for Self-Awareness

Reflection exercises and journaling are effective techniques for developing self-awareness because they provide people with a methodical and perceptive means of examining their feelings, ideas, and experiences. We will explore the advantages and methods of integrating journaling and reflecting activities into everyday living in this part.

- **The Journaling Power:**

The ancient practice of journaling entails keeping a regular log of one's thoughts and experiences. This written investigation offers a concrete means of self-expression and self-exploration. Writing down one's thoughts enables a

- more in-depth interaction with them and promotes a higher degree of self-awareness.

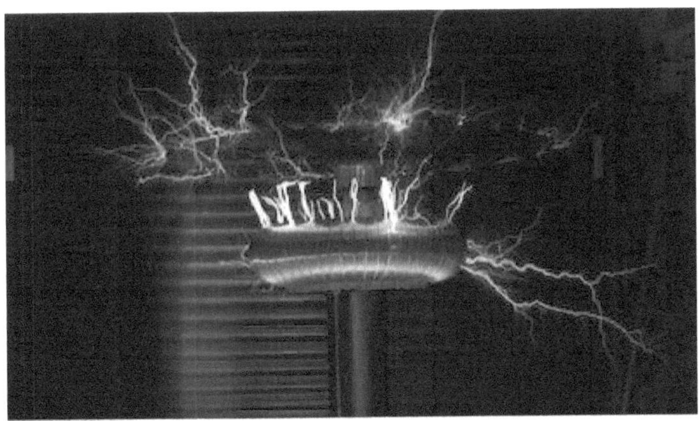

- **Journaling Based on Emotions:**

Make time in your journal to write about your feelings. Throughout the day, describe your feelings, taking note of any patterns or mood swings. This exercise facilitates the identification of emotional triggers and the comprehension of the variables affecting your emotional terrain.

○ **Journaling Your Gratitude**: Keep a thankfulness notebook to help you concentrate on the good things in your life. Write down your blessings on a regular basis. By increasing your awareness of the positive aspects of your life and building resilience in the face of adversity, this practice helps you develop a positive mentality.

○ **Writing in the Stream of Consciousness:** Let your ideas come to you without restriction while you write. This writing is an uncensored stream of consciousness that may expose wants, fears, or subconscious ideas. It offers an unvarnished and sincere glimpse into your inner life.

● **Journal for Setting Goals:** Incorporate self-awareness into goal-setting by outlining your long- and short-term objectives. Think back on the steps you take to achieve these objectives and the feelings you had at each turn. This kind of journaling strengthens the link between your feelings and your goals for yourself.

● **Introspective Tasks:** Make a timeline that highlights the important moments in your life. Consider the feelings evoked by each incident and look for any trends or recurring themes. This activity gives you a holistic perspective of your life journey and helps you understand how your emotions from the past have shaped your feelings now.

○ **Emotional SWOT Analysis:** Customize the SWOT analysis (Strengths, Weaknesses, Opportunities, Threats) to your emotional terrain from a commercial perspective. Recognize your emotional assets, admit your shortcomings, look for chances to develop emotionally, and identify any dangers to your emotional health.

○ **Writing a Letter:** Whether you plan to send them or not, write letters to yourself or others. In these letters, share your feelings, goals, and complaints. This practice gives an emotional outlet that is beneficial and sheds light on unsaid ideas.

○ **Reflection Questions for Each Day:** At the end of each day, ask yourself some introspective questions. "What emotions did I experience today?" is one example. "How did I respond to challenging situations?" "What can I learn from today's experiences?" Self-awareness is improved through regular introspection using focused inquiries.

● **Advantages of Reflection and Journaling: - Enhanced Self-Awareness:** Your comprehension of your ideas and feelings will deepen with regular journaling and reflection. Your increased self-awareness enables you to make wise choices that are consistent with your moral principles.

○ **Reduction of Stress:** It has been demonstrated that verbalizing feelings lowers stress and improves emotional health. Pent-up emotions can be constructively processed and released through journaling.

● **Ease and Concentration:** Your objectives, morals, and feelings become more clear when you engage in reflective practices. More deliberate decisions and daily actions are made easier by this increased clarity.

Improved Capabilities for Solving Problems: Maintaining a journal enables you to evaluate obstacles and failures with objectivity. This analytical method develops your ability to solve problems by assisting you in determining practical approaches to problems.

Individual Development: Journaling eventually becomes a log of your own personal progress. Examining previous entries provides insight into one's development, identifies areas for growth, and provides inspiration for ongoing self-improvement.

A regimen that includes writing and reflection exercises gives you a systematic framework for developing self-awareness. These routines serve as mirrors, reflecting the complex terrain of your ideas and feelings. You build emotional intelligence by participating in this continuous process of self-discovery, which opens the door to additional development in later stages of your journey.

2.4 Mindfulness Practices for Heightened Self-Awareness

Higher self-awareness is cultivated through mindfulness activities, which are essential to the development of emotional intelligence. By deliberately focusing on the present moment with no judgment, mindfulness enables people to notice their thoughts and feelings without getting caught up in them. The many mindfulness practices and their significant influence on self-awareness are examined in this section.

- **Breath Awareness Meditation:** - Take a comfortable seat at the beginning and concentrate on your breathing.

  0 Take note of your breathing's natural rhythm and the rise and fall of your abdomen or chest.

  ○ Gently return your attention to the breath whenever thoughts come up, without passing judgment.

Awareness of Breath A fundamental mindfulness practice is meditation. People can learn to notice the rise and fall of their thoughts and feelings by training their attention to be anchored in their breathing. It is from this increased awareness that patterns and triggers can be identified.

- **Body Scan Meditation:** - Take a comfortable seat or lie down, and focus your attention on various body areas.

  0 Carefully examine every region, noting any feelings without passing judgment.

○ By encouraging a greater awareness of emotional and physical states, this practice strengthens the bond between the mind and body.

By focusing attention on bodily sensations, the body scan meditation improves self-awareness and provides insights into how emotions appear in the body. The ability to identify and comprehend emotional reactions is aided by this increased body awareness.

- **Mindful Eating:** - Give your entire attention to the act of eating.
0 Take note of the tastes, textures, and colors of every bite.
○ Be mindful of how it feels to chew and swallow.

The concepts of mindful eating are applied to everyday tasks. People can cultivate a more mindful relationship with their eating habits and, consequently, their emotional reactions to food by practicing mindfulness during meals.

- **Sensory Awareness:** - Take a moment to concentrate on using all of your senses.

0 Take note of the surrounding sights, sounds, tastes, smells, and textures.

○ By encouraging a sharp awareness of one's surroundings, this practice helps one project a grounded, centering presence.

Awareness of senses People can better connect with their immediate surroundings by practicing mindfulness. People who actively use their senses to anchor themselves in the present moment clear out their minds and become more self-aware.

● **Love-Kindness Meditation:** - Direct your well-wishes towards yourself and other people in order to cultivate feelings of compassion and love.

0 Start with yourself, then move on to your family, friends, and even those you may not get along with.

○ By cultivating empathy and compassion, this exercise extends one's understanding of their own emotional reactions and interpersonal interactions.

Kindness and love Through the cultivation of compassion for both oneself and others, meditation, or "metta," fosters a more self-aware perspective. Through cultivating pleasant emotions, people can learn more about their own empathy and understanding abilities.

● **Thought Labeling:** - Examine your ideas objectively and without bias.

0 As ideas come to you, classify them as neutral, negative, or good.

○ By distancing oneself from thoughts, this practice enables people to witness their thoughts without becoming engulfed in them.

A mindfulness practice called "thought labeling" helps people become more self-aware by establishing a framework for unbiased mental observation of their thoughts. People can better understand the nature and frequency of particular mental patterns by classifying their thoughts.

Daily Check-Ins with Mindfulness:

○ Designate particular periods of the day for quick mindfulness check-ins.

○ Take a moment to stop and focus on your feelings, ideas, and physical experiences.

Make the most of these opportunities to check in with yourself and your emotional condition.

Short mindfulness check-ins might be a useful strategy to maintain elevated self-awareness in everyday tasks. People are better able to handle everyday obstacles with more emotional intelligence when they take these deliberate breaks.

● **Mindful Walking:** - Take a brisk stroll while focusing on each stride and the feeling of movement.

0 As you walk, pay attention to the surroundings and the minute changes in your body.

○ Walking mindfully is a way to incorporate mindfulness with physical exercise, encouraging a comprehensive approach to self-awareness.

Walking mindfully cultivates a link between the body and the mind by integrating awareness with movement. By encouraging people to pay attention to their external environment and interior experiences, this practice helps people become more self-aware generally.

Increased Self-Awareness with Mindfulness Practices:

● **Improved Emotional Regulation:** By helping people to notice their emotions as they emerge, mindfulness techniques help people respond to difficult circumstances in a more deliberate and measured manner.

0 Improved Stress Handling: By encouraging a non-reactive awareness of thoughts and emotions, regular mindfulness practice lowers stress and increases people's resilience in the face of stressors.

- **Enhanced Focus and Concentration:** Mindfulness improves cognitive processes, which results in heightened awareness and better focus throughout everyday tasks.

- **Enhanced Clarity of Emotions:** People can better comprehend their emotional environment and identify triggers and trends by detachedly monitoring their thoughts and feelings.

- **Increased Mind-Body Harmony:** Holistic self-awareness is fostered by mindfulness activities, especially those that involve the body and strengthen the link between emotional moods and physical sensations.

- **Compassion Cultivation:** Loving-kindness meditation fosters empathy for both oneself and other people by cultivating a compassionate viewpoint.

Developing a daily practice of mindfulness offers a revolutionary route to increased self-awareness. Through practicing mindfulness and adopting an accepting perspective towards one's inner experiences, people prepare themselves for the next stages of emotional intelligence growth. Frequent participation in these practices builds a strong foundation for navigating the intricacies of emotions and promotes a thorough understanding of oneself.

2.5 Exploring Personal Values and Beliefs

Investigating one's own values and beliefs is a crucial part of developing emotional intelligence. Being aware of the fundamental ideas that direct our behavior and thinking is essential to becoming self-aware. This chapter explores the importance of investigating values and beliefs and provides recommendations on how to proceed with this self-reflection.

- **Outlining Personal Principles:** - Our objectives and decision-making processes are shaped by our own values, which serve as guiding principles. They stand for the things in life that we value and find significant.

0 Think about the areas of life that truly speak to you as you start to examine your values. Think about concepts like connection, achievement, compassion, and integrity.

Comprehending one's own values serves as a basis for coordinating activities with internal priorities. By recognizing and embracing these values, people become more aware of the motivations behind their decisions and actions.

○ **Contemplating Belief Systems:**

Belief systems are the collections of views and convictions that influence how we perceive the outside world, ourselves, and other people.

○ Consider your views on a range of topics, including morality, relationships, achievement, and meaning in life. Think about the impacts these beliefs have been shaped by.

Analyzing belief systems reveals the lenses through which we view the world, which in turn promotes self-awareness. Understanding where these ideas came from enables people to evaluate their applicability and validity in the present.

- **Alignment with Actions:** - After determining your values and beliefs, assess the degree to which they are in line with your decisions and behaviors.

0 Think about the situations where your actions might not be consistent with your principles. This discrepancy may point out opportunities for reflection and personal development.

Living genuinely requires coordinating actions with values. People feel a sense of integrity and coherence when their actions are consistent with their personal values, which enhances emotional wellbeing.

● Prioritizing Values: Sort your values according to significance. This ranking makes it clear which values are more important while making decisions.

0 Be aware that moral principles can change throughout time. Consistently reevaluating and rearranging values facilitates continuous self-exploration.

Setting values first helps people make choices that are consistent with their basic beliefs. It facilitates decision-making in complex settings by offering a distinct hierarchy of values.

● **Value-Based Decision-Making:** - Make decisions by using your values as a guide. When presented with options, think about how each option relates to your basic beliefs.

0 By encouraging deliberate decision-making, this strategy lessens the possibility of regrets or internal conflicts.

A sense of direction and purpose is fostered when decisions are made based on values. It offers a dependable framework for overcoming obstacles in life and remaining loyal to oneself.

● **Examination of Social and Cultural Factors:**

0 Consider the ways in which society and culture have influenced your values and opinions.

○ Think about if particular ideals are a part of your unique identity or if they are shaped by other forces.

Individuals can distinguish between values that are imposed by outside forces and those that are intrinsic when they acknowledge the influence of culture and society on personal values. The development of a more genuine and deeply meaningful value system is aided by this knowledge.

Using mindfulness techniques to the investigation of values is * **Mindfulness in Value Exploration:**. Consider how your values affect your feelings, ideas, and actions on a regular basis.

• Develop an understanding of values in a variety of spheres of life, such as relationships, work, and personal growth.

In value inquiry, mindfulness entails monitoring values' effects in real time. People can have a deeper knowledge of how values appear in all facets of life and modify them in response to evolving situations by integrating mindfulness.

• **Values in Relationships:** - Consider how the values of the important people in your life coincide with your own.

0 Acknowledge that while divergent values may necessitate compromise and open communication, similar values support harmonious partnerships.

Relationships are healthier when people are able to comprehend one another's values and have an honest discussion about shared values. It enables people to resolve possible disputes amicably and sympathetically.

• **Ongoing Introspection and Adjustment:**

0 Continue to consider your principles and convictions. Value changes can be brought about by human development and life events.

○ As you grow, be willing to modify your values so that they continue to accurately represent who you are.

A dynamic and changing self-awareness is supported by ongoing introspection and value modification. In addition to fostering personal development, this approach guarantees that values are applicable and significant throughout one's lifetime.

Personal Values and Beliefs Exploration Benefits:

○ Enhanced Awareness of Oneself:** Examining values and beliefs reveals the underlying principles that underpin attitudes and actions, which enhances self-awareness.

● Better Decision-Making: Making decisions that are in line with one's personal values offers a lucid and consistent foundation for choosing actions that are true to oneself.

● **Higher Emotional Resilience:** By offering a solid basis for overcoming obstacles and disappointments, an understanding of values enhances emotional resilience.

● **Authentic Living:** Leading a life that is consistent with one's ideals creates authenticity and encourages everyday fulfillment and a sense of purpose.

● **Improved Interpersonal Relationships:** A deeper and more meaningful connection with people is facilitated by the recognition and alignment of values in relationships.

● **Adaptability to Change:** Constant introspection and value adaption promote flexibility in reaction to shifting conditions, allowing for a more seamless passage through life's transitions.

Investigating one's own values and beliefs is a continuous process of reflection and self-discovery. People establish the foundation for growing emotional intelligence and negotiating the complexity of their own inner terrain with more clarity and honesty by exploring the fundamental ideas that direct our life.

Chapter 3: Developing Self-Regulation

3.1 Strategies for Managing and Controlling Emotions

An understanding of emotions is the first step toward good emotion regulation. Emotions are signals that tell us what we need and how to react in different circumstances. The first step in becoming emotionally intelligent is learning to identify and accept your feelings.

Techniques for Regulating Emotions:

The emphasis then turns to controlling emotions after they have been recognized. Creating strategies to control the strength and duration of feelings is known as emotion regulation. For example, deep breathing exercises can assist lower elevated emotional states and relax the nervous system.

Notes and Contemplation:

Maintaining a journal offers a disciplined approach to consider and work through feelings. People have the ability to analyze patterns, pinpoint triggers, and investigate the underlying causes of their emotions. Self-analysis like this promotes emotional awareness and aids in the creation of unique emotional management techniques.

Identifying Triggers: It's important to know what sets off particular emotional reactions. People can actively control their reactions by identifying the circumstances or stimuli that cause strong emotions. This could entail avoiding triggers wherever feasible or using coping methods in the event that stimuli cannot be avoided.

Psycho-Somatic Link:

The secret to controlling emotions is understanding how the mind and body are related. A balanced diet, regular exercise, and enough sleep all improve general wellbeing and have a favorable impact on emotional states. The ability to properly handle stress and emotional difficulties is improved by physical well-being.

Looking for Social Assistance:

Since humans are social creatures, asking friends, family, or coworkers for support can be very helpful in controlling emotions. Talking to people about how you feel offers you a variety of viewpoints and possible answers in addition to a release for your emotions.

Determining Limits:

Emotional health depends on the establishment of sound boundaries. This entails being aware of one's boundaries and properly communicating them. A more lasting emotional balance is facilitated by learning when and how to say "no," as well as by placing a high priority on self-care.

Developing Positive Habits: Taking part in joyful and fulfilling activities elevates one's emotional condition. One way to combat bad emotions and promote resilience is to engage in hobbies, express gratitude, and schedule in happy moments.

Expert Assistance:

It is a wise decision to seek professional assistance when feelings become unbearable or persistent. Counselors and therapists can offer direction, impart new coping mechanisms, and create a safe space where people can explore and comprehend their feelings.

Ongoing Education and Adjustment:

Managing emotions is a lifelong process that calls for constant learning and adjustment. People ought to be willing to learn new tactics, hone those they already have, and modify their methods in response to changing self-awareness and life events.

To sum up, developing emotional intelligence greatly benefits from a lifetime of practice in the discipline of emotion management and control. By using these techniques, people can develop self-regulation, which will improve their relationships, well-being, and ability to succeed in both their personal and professional efforts. The goal of developing emotional intelligence is to comprehend, accept, and skillfully navigate the complex web of human emotions rather than to repress them.

3.2 Mindfulness and Stress Management Techniques

To be well overall, one must be able to handle stress and develop a thoughtful approach to living in the fast-paced, frequently chaotic modern world. In-depth discussions of the significant effects of stress reduction and mindfulness on emotional intelligence are provided in this part, along with helpful tips for incorporating these practices into everyday life.

A Knowledge of Mindfulness:

The practice of mindfulness has its roots in antiquated contemplative traditions and is becoming increasingly well-known in modern situations. Fundamentally, practicing mindfulness is learning to live in the present moment with intention and without passing judgment. This awareness creates a strong bond with one's inner experiences by encompassing ideas, feelings, and sensations.

Meditation with Mindfulness:

Meditation is one of the core techniques of mindfulness. By gently directing the mind back when it wanders, mindfulness meditation encourages people to focus their attention on their breath, physical sensations, or a particular focused point. Frequent practice increases awareness, decreases daydreaming, and improves attention.

Progressive Muscle Relaxation and Body Scan:

Beyond meditation, mindfulness can be used for methods like progressive muscle relaxation and body scanning. During a body scan, various body areas are methodically brought into focus, encouraging relaxation and an understanding of one's own body's sensations. By tensing and then relaxing various muscle groups, progressive muscle relaxation helps to ease physical tension and foster calmness.

Cognitive Inhalation:

Mindfulness is based on the principle of attentive breathing. Breathing deeply, slowly, and deliberately calms the central nervous system. It facilitates a transition from the sympathetic nervous system, which raises tension, to the parasympathetic nervous system, which lowers stress and increases feelings of calm.

Conscientious Strolling and Motion:

Being mindful may be integrated into activity as well as stillness. Walking mindfully entails focusing on the feelings in your feet, the surroundings, and every step you take. Other forms of mindful movement include yoga and tai chi, which combine physical exercise with an increased awareness of one's body and breath.

Practicing Mindfulness in Everyday Tasks:

By incorporating mindfulness into daily work, regular tasks become chances to practice present and awareness. People can practice being totally present in the moment when eating, cleaning up after themselves, or traveling, which will lower stress and improve the quality of their experiences.

MBSR, or mindfulness-based stress reduction:

MBSR is an organized program that incorporates mindfulness meditation and awareness into everyday living. It was created by Dr.

Jon Kabat-Zinn. It has proven to have positive effects on emotional well-being and has been widely accepted as an effective stress reduction strategy.

Acceptance and Commitment Therapy (ACT): Based on mindfulness, ACT is a therapy technique that prioritizes acceptance of ideas and feelings over their eradication. It promotes people to make their values clear and take decisive action, which builds psychological flexibility and resilience in the face of adversity.

Technology and Mindfulness Applications:

Many mindfulness apps and technology provide easily accessible methods to integrate mindfulness into everyday life in the digital age. With the help of these tools, which frequently offer breathing exercises, progress tracking, and guided meditations, people with hectic schedules can more easily adopt mindfulness practices.

Emotional Intelligence and Mindfulness:

Emotional intelligence and mindfulness practices are closely related. People who practice mindfulness of their thoughts and feelings are better able to react to circumstances with more purpose and clarity. Being mindful makes it possible to pause between being stimulated and responding, which permits more deliberate and controlled responses.

Stress Reduction Methods:

Although stress will always be a part of life, mental health depends on learning how to effectively manage it. Time management, realistic goal-setting, and task prioritization are some strategies that help people feel in control and less likely to feel overwhelmed.

Stress Management Through Mindfulness:

The effectiveness of stress management strategies is increased when mindfulness is incorporated. When pressures are mindfully recognized and intentional reactions are made, people are better equipped to handle difficulties with resilience and poise.

Individuals and Awareness:

Making a connection with nature is an effective way to reduce stress. It has been demonstrated that spending time outside, whether in a park or other natural setting, lowers stress levels and fosters a sense of calm.

Developing an Intentional Way of Living:

The ultimate objective is to develop a mindful lifestyle in which being aware is an organic and integrated part of day-to-day existence. Self-compassion, consistent practice, and a dedication to being present in every moment of life are required for this.

To sum up, practicing stress reduction and mindfulness are crucial skills for developing emotional intelligence. People can improve their ability to manage stress and develop a better knowledge of their feelings, ideas, and actions by adopting these activities into their daily lives. The path to emotional intelligence is enhanced by practicing mindfulness, which encourages a harmonious union of the body, mind, and spirit in the fabric of life.

3.3 Building Resilience and Emotional Stability

Building emotional stability and resilience becomes crucial in the complex dance of life, where obstacles and doubts are unavoidable. This section delves into the mutually beneficial relationship between emotional stability and resilience, elucidating the tactics and frame of mind that foster long-lasting fortitude in the face of hardship.

A Knowledge of Resilience:

Resilience is the capacity to overcome obstacles with a feeling of mastery, adjust to change, and recover from failures. It is sometimes compared to a buoyant spirit. It's about building the ability to deal with life's inevitable challenges, not about avoiding them. Those who are resilient have a mental and emotional fortitude that enables them to hold onto hope and a sense of purpose during trying times.

Developing a Growth Mentality:

The development of a growth mindset lies at the foundation of resilience building. This way of thinking, made popular by psychologist

Carol Dweck, is based on the conviction that aptitude and intellect can be acquired with commitment and diligence. People who have a growth mentality see setbacks as chances for growth and learning instead of as insurmountable roadblocks. This way of looking at things gives people the ability to accept challenges, grow from mistakes, and keep going when things become tough.

Acceptance and Self-Compassion:

Self-acceptance and self-compassion are the foundations of resilience. Resilient people treat themselves with respect and acknowledge their humanity, practicing self-compassion instead of punishing themselves severely for any flaws they may have. An essential component of emotional stability is learning to accept one's strengths and weaknesses.

Creating a Helpful Network:

Resilience greatly benefits from social ties. Having a solid support system of friends, family, and coworkers offers a safety net in trying times. Emotional stability is strengthened and a sense of belonging is fostered by asking for help and sharing experiences.

Adaptive Coping Strategies: When faced with challenges, resilient people use adaptive coping techniques. These tactics could involve fixing problems, getting perspective, and rephrasing difficulties. Resilient people take a proactive, solution-focused approach to problems rather than giving in to hopelessness.

Gratitude Verses and Affirmations:

It is impossible to overestimate the effectiveness of visualization and positive affirmations in fostering resilience. Affirmations support and strengthen a feeling of self-efficacy and a good self-image. Visualization techniques help people develop a resilient and optimistic mindset by having them mentally practice successful outcomes.

Growing from Misfortune:

Resilience is the ability to overcome hardship and learn from it as well as to bounce back. Personal development is facilitated by thinking back on difficult situations and drawing important lessons from them. People who are resilient use setbacks as a chance for personal growth and self-discovery.

Courage in the Face of Difficulties:

One of the main elements of resilience is the practice of mindfulness. Being mindful helps people to stop worrying needlessly about the future or focusing on difficult memories from the past. In the face of difficulties, emotional stability is facilitated by this present-focused awareness.

Control of Emotions:

The capacity to successfully control and regulate emotions is a prerequisite for emotional stability, which goes hand in hand with resilience. Instead of ignoring or suppressing their feelings, resilient people approach things with awareness and a sense of control. A steady and well-balanced mental state is facilitated by this emotional control.

Setting Realistic Goals: People who are resilient make attainable goals. These objectives give guidance and meaning, acting as guiding lights amid trying circumstances. Larger tasks can be broken down into smaller steps to help people feel like they're making progress.

Preserving Physical Health:

There is a close relationship between the mind and body, and emotional stability depends on physical health. Sufficient sleep, consistent physical activity, and a nutritious diet promote the best possible cognitive and emotional functioning, which in turn enhances resilience overall.

Developing an Optimism:

One of the most important components of resilience is optimism, or the conviction that good things are achievable. Reframing negative thoughts, emphasizing strengths, and keeping a positive attitude in the midst of difficulty are all part of cultivating optimism.

Lifelong Learning and Professional Development:

Resilience is fostered by supporting lifelong learning and making investments in professional growth. Learning new things improves flexibility and boosts self-assurance when facing a variety of obstacles in the personal and professional spheres.

Looking for Expert Assistance:

It takes resilience to ask for expert help when facing extreme hardship. Counselors, therapists, and support groups offer a secure environment where people can examine their feelings, acquire understanding, and create coping mechanisms.

In short, developing emotional stability and resilience is a continuous process that closely relates to the growth of emotional intelligence. Being resilient is a skill that may be developed and enhanced over time rather than a set attribute. Through embracing a growth mindset, engaging in self-compassion exercises, and utilizing flexible coping mechanisms, people can improve their ability to handle the challenges of life with resilience and elegance. The process of developing emotional stability and resilience is transformational, enabling people to face difficulties head-on, grow from misfortune, and come out stronger on the other side.

3.4 Cognitive Restructuring for Emotional Control

The capacity to manage and control one's emotions is a basic competency in the complex field of emotional intelligence. A treatment strategy based on cognitive-behavioral concepts called cognitive restructuring shows promise as a potent instrument for improving emotional regulation. This section delves into the idea of cognitive restructuring and how it can be used to rewire thought patterns in order to produce more positive emotional results.

A Comprehensive Overview of Cognitive Restructuring:

A psychological procedure called cognitive restructuring, sometimes referred to as cognitive reframing or cognitive-behavioral restructuring, tries to recognize and alter unfavorable thought patterns. It is predicated on the notion that our thoughts shape our feelings and actions. Through the process of reframing and confronting maladaptive thought patterns, people are able to modify their emotional reactions and, in turn, their overall condition.

Identifying Thought Patterns That Are Negative

Finding harmful thought patterns is the first stage in the cognitive restructuring process. These tendencies frequently show themselves as cognitive distortions, which are biased and unreasonable ways of thinking that exacerbate unpleasant feelings. Catastrophizing, thinking in black and white, and personalizing are examples of common distortions.

Fighting Cognitive Illusions:

The next stage is to confront and refute negative thought patterns after they have been identified. People must challenge the veracity and accuracy of their ideas during this process. Someone who frequently imagines the worst-case scenario in any circumstance, for instance, may be challenged by weighing the arguments for and against such catastrophic thinking.

Changing the Way You Think:

The emphasis moves from confronting negative thoughts to rephrasing them in a realistic and balanced manner. This entails replacing illogical ideas with more sensible and beneficial ones. Reframing promotes a change in perspective from one that is more empowering and uplifting to one that is negative and self-defeating.

Emotional Regulation and Cognitive Restructuring:

There is a strong correlation between emotional regulation and cognitive reorganization. People can better regulate their emotional reactions when they learn to identify and confront problematic thought patterns. The goal of this technique is to change how emotions are perceived and expressed rather than to suppress them.

Automatic Mind Tracking:

One method of cognitive restructuring is automatic thought monitoring, which is observing ideas that come to mind on their own when faced with a specific circumstance. By keeping an eye on these automatic thoughts, people can spot trends and act quickly to reframe ideas before they develop into strong feelings.

Diaries and Mental Notes:

One useful method of putting cognitive restructuring into practice is to keep a thought journal or use thought logs. People have the ability to document their ideas, related feelings, and the situations that gave rise to these ideas. This introspective procedure makes it easier to recognize cognitive distortions and offers a well-organized framework for reorganization.

Cognitive restructuring and mindfulness:

Emotional control is improved when mindfulness exercises are combined with cognitive restructuring. People who practice mindfulness are more inclined to notice their thoughts in the here and now, without passing judgment. This awareness makes room for cognitive reorganization, which enables people to react to ideas more deliberately.

Restructuring Your Mind and Talking to Yourself:

The internal conversation people have with themselves, or self-talk, has a big impact on how they feel. Cognitive restructuring entails changing self-defeating statements to more uplifting and encouraging ones. This change in self-talk promotes a more positive and emotionally stable way of thinking.

The Role of Core ideas: Cognitive restructuring explores people's deeply held, fundamental ideas about the world, other people, and themselves. People can address the underlying causes of negative thought patterns and make significant and long-lasting changes in their emotional responses by questioning and rearranging their essential beliefs.

Sequential Exposure and Cognitive Reorganization:

Cognitive restructuring in conjunction with gradual exposure can be very helpful when people are dealing with worries or concerns. Gradual exposure refers to methodically and gradually facing fearful situations. This process is complemented by cognitive restructuring, which deals with and modifies the negative beliefs connected to the fearful situations.

Expert Counseling and Cognitive Reorganization:

Although cognitive restructuring can be used as a self-help technique, getting expert advice increases its efficacy. Cognitive-behavioral therapy (CBT) educated therapists can offer individualized approaches, direction, and assistance in the cognitive restructuring process.

Application in Everyday Life:

Cognitive restructuring must be incorporated throughout daily life in order to have a transforming effect. By practicing consistently, even in ordinary or routine circumstances, people can strengthen their ability to resist negative thought patterns and improve their emotional regulation in a variety of contexts.

Emotional Intelligence Long-Term Effects:

Cognitive restructuring has a significant long-term effect on emotional intelligence. People who regularly use these methods not only become more adept at managing their emotions, but they also become more self-aware and emotionally resilient. In the process of developing emotional intelligence more broadly, cognitive restructuring turns into a fundamental ability.

To sum up, cognitive restructuring is a powerful tool for gaining emotional control over oneself. People can modify their emotional experiences by methodically recognizing, disputing, and reframing unfavorable thought patterns. This procedure not only enhances emotional intelligence but also promotes a more upbeat and flexible attitude toward life's obstacles. Cognitive restructuring is a transformative tool that helps people traverse their inner landscapes more clearly, which improves emotional well-being and builds resilience in the mind.

3.5 Enhancing Emotional Intelligence through Relaxation Techniques

The incorporation of relaxation techniques presents itself as a transformative pathway in the complex process of cultivating emotional intelligence. This section delves into the significant influence of relaxation techniques on augmenting emotional intelligence. It offers perspectives on the ways in which techniques like progressive muscle relaxation, deep breathing, and meditation support emotional wellness.

Understanding Relaxation and Emotional Intelligence:

Relaxation techniques are a natural ally of emotional intelligence, which is commonly defined as the capacity to identify, comprehend, and regulate one's own emotions while skillfully navigating interpersonal relationships. Fundamentally, relaxation is a condition of mental and emotional serenity that serves as the basis for improved social skills and emotional management. It goes beyond simple physical rest.

Mindfulness and Meditation Techniques:

The key to improving emotional intelligence through relaxing is to practice mindfulness and meditation. In order to meditate, one must turn within, frequently concentrating on the breath, thoughts, or feelings. An essential element of meditation is mindfulness, which stresses non-judgmental awareness of the current moment. Higher levels of self-awareness and emotional control are developed with regular practice.

Intense Breathing Techniques:

The foundation of relaxation techniques consists of deep breathing exercises that are simple yet effective. Intentional, slow, and deep breathing is used in techniques like diaphragmatic breathing and box breathing. The parasympathetic nervous system is triggered by deep breathing, which reduces stress and encourages relaxation.

Muscular relaxation with progressive muscles:

Progressive muscle relaxation is a methodical approach that entails consciously tensing and relaxing several muscle groups in turn. This procedure increases awareness of internal stress while simultaneously promoting physical relaxation. People who practice PMR become more adept at releasing physical stress, which promotes emotional balance.

Guided Imagery and Visualization: Techniques for guided imagery and visualization make use of the mind's ability to conjure up peaceful, serene mental images. These techniques use the imagination to create a relaxing mood, whether it is via imagining a peaceful natural location or a successful outcome. Emotional intelligence benefits from this mental break.

Tai Chi and Yoga:

Meditation, controlled breathing, and physical postures are all incorporated into mind-body disciplines like yoga and tai chi. It has been demonstrated that both improve self-awareness, lessen stress, and support emotional health. These activities' deliberate movement cultivates a feeling of equilibrium and centering, which is consistent with the objectives of emotional intelligence.

Autonomous Instruction:

Self-suggestions used in autogenic training lead to a relaxed condition. Repeating words that conjure feelings of warmth and weight can help people induce a peaceful and tranquil body reaction. By improving the body-mind link, this method fosters emotional balance and aids in the growth of emotional intelligence.

Biofeedback:

A technology-assisted relaxation approach called biofeedback gives people instantaneous information about physiological processes like skin temperature, muscle tension, and heart rate. People can improve their capacity to control their emotions and stress by learning to master these physiological reactions. Biofeedback is consistent with emotional intelligence's self-awareness component.

Emotional Intelligence and Mind-Body Techniques:

Including mind-body exercises in everyday activities improves emotional awareness. During relaxation exercises, people get a more sophisticated awareness of their emotional states by focusing on their breath, thoughts, and physical sensations. Emotional intelligence is based on this acute sensitivity.

Depression Alleviation and Emotional Sturdiness:

The ability of relaxation techniques to reduce stress plays a crucial role in developing emotional resilience. Sustained stress can affect one's ability to regulate emotions, increasing one's susceptibility to unpleasant feelings. Regular relaxation training serves as a protective barrier, promoting emotional stability and mitigating the negative consequences of stress.

Building Interpersonal Relationships: Relaxation improves emotional intelligence, which in turn builds interpersonal relationships. Empathetic understanding, productive dispute resolution, and successful communication are all facilitated by maintaining composure and centering oneself. In social situations, those who are at ease tend to react more thoughtfully than impulsively.

Reliability and Adaptability to Everyday Life:

Consistency and integration into everyday life are prerequisites for the effectiveness of relaxation techniques in boosting emotional intelligence. Short relaxation techniques can be incorporated into regular activities to give people readily available tools for stress management and mood regulation. Long-term emotional intelligence development is facilitated by consistent practice.

Workplace Utilization:

In the workplace, relaxation methods are used to improve emotional intelligence.

Employers are beginning to understand the value of stress reduction and wellness initiatives, using relaxation techniques to help staff members build emotional resilience and promote a healthy work atmosphere.

Advise and Instruction:

Although many relaxation methods may be learned on your own, their efficacy is increased when you use structured programs or seek the advice of qualified experts. Participants in guided relaxation sessions or mindfulness-based stress reduction (MBSR) training acquire the abilities and information necessary to successfully incorporate these practices.

A Comprehensive Perspective on Emotional Intelligence:

The comprehensive aspect of this development is highlighted by the integration of relaxation techniques within the emotional intelligence journey. Understanding and controlling emotions is only one aspect of emotional intelligence; another is building a foundation of wellbeing that enables people to face obstacles in life with poise and fortitude.

In summary, developing emotional intelligence with relaxing methods is a liberating and uplifting experience. People establish the foundation for self-awareness, emotional control, and healthy interpersonal connections by developing a steady and composed mind. By incorporating these strategies into daily life, people can develop their emotional intelligence and cultivate a comprehensive feeling of well-being that enables them to succeed in both their personal and professional lives.

Chapter 4: Motivation and Goal Setting

4.1 Understanding Intrinsic and Extrinsic Motivation

Human behavior is driven by motivation, which inspires people to set and accomplish goals, overcome obstacles, and succeed. Intrinsic and extrinsic motivation are two separate but related factors that influence human behavior in the field of motivation. This section explores the subtleties of several sources of motivation and how they affect behavior, output, and general well-being.

Intellectual Drive:

Internal causes are the source of intrinsic motivation; people are motivated by their own interests, desires, or the intrinsic satisfaction that comes from doing something. This type of motivation is derived from the pure happiness, inquisitiveness, or sense of accomplishment that comes from completing a certain job. People are motivated to act by their own intrinsic rewards and enjoyment of the task itself. This is known as intrinsic motivation.

Intrinsic Motivation Characteristics:

1. **Legal Independence:** An atmosphere that grants people a sense of independence and self-direction is conducive to the growth of intrinsic drive. Intrinsic motivation thrives in situations where people are free to decide for themselves what to do.

2. **Passion and Interest:** Engaging in activities that a person is passionate about and interested in can be a great way to find intrinsic motivation. The intrinsic satisfaction that these kinds of activities provide serves as the impetus for consistent effort and involvement.

3. **Difficulty and Expertise:** The quest for mastery and the pursuit of challenges are intimately related to intrinsic motivation. Intrinsically motivated people look for challenges that push them beyond their comfort zones and present chances for professional and personal development.

4. **Enjoyment of the Process:** For those who are genuinely motivated, the act of participating in an activity itself becomes enjoyable. In addition to reaching their objectives, they derive satisfaction from the process and the encounters encountered along the way.

5. **Contentment within:** For those that are intrinsically motivated, the main benefits come from the internal fulfillment and sense of achievement they get from their work. The intrinsic delight of the activity takes precedence above any external accolades or rewards.

Intrinsic Motivation Examples:

1. **Education for the Purpose of Education:** Intrinsic motivation is demonstrated by someone who pursues knowledge or skills purely for the purpose of personal development and learning.

2. **Artistic Expression:** People who are passionate about

creating art, music, or writing frequently show intrinsic motivation in their work.

3. **Activities and Sports:** People who participate in sports or physical activities for the enjoyment of the activity, the challenge, or the personal fulfillment are prime examples of intrinsic motivation.

4. **Problem-Solving:** The quest for answers to difficult puzzles or difficulties purely for the sake of intellectual stimulation and fulfillment is indicative of intrinsic drive.

Motivation from Without:

Conversely, extrinsic motivation arises from outside sources like incentives, acknowledgment, or penalties. Extrinsically motivated people participate in things more for the external rewards or outcomes than for the intrinsic enjoyment of the activity itself. These outside elements function as a stimulant for actions and output.

Extrinsic Motivation Characteristics:

1. **Additional Benefits:** Extrinsic drive is frequently associated with material gains like cash, accolades, grades, or other types of acknowledgment. These outside rewards function as outside reinforcement for carrying out a certain action.

2. Steer clear of punishment: An effective extrinsic motivation can be the desire to avoid punishment or unfavorable outcomes. People could participate in an activity to avoid unfavorable consequences.

3. **Social Validation:** The desire for recognition, acceptance, or approval from others can be the source of extrinsic motivation. Behavior is driven by other people's recognition and external affirmation.

4. **Road opposition:** One type of extrinsic motivation is the competitive drive, which is sparked by the desire to perform better than others or achieve a higher position.

5. **monetary Gains:** Seeking monetary advantages in the workplace and other contexts, such as bonuses, promotions, or belongings, can be powerful extrinsic motivators.

Instances of Motivation from Without:

1. **Financial Rewards at Work:** Extrinsic considerations related to money gain drive employees who strive for a salary, bonuses, or promotion.
2. **Educational Grades:** Extrinsic drive related to academic performance influences students who study for excellent marks and recognition in the classroom.
3. **Sports Competition:** The extrinsic motivation of winning a competition and receiving acclaim from others drives athletes aiming for medals, trophies, or records.
4. **Employee Recognition Programs:** These are workplace campaigns aimed at utilizing extrinsic incentive. They provide employees rewards, recognition, or titles such as employee of the month.

Interaction between External and Internal Motivation:

Despite the common misconception that intrinsic and extrinsic motivation are separate, they regularly interact and have an impact on one another. An individual's total motivation landscape can be shaped by the dynamic interactions between different motivating factors.

Combined Regulation: Extrinsic motivators may be internalized by people and transformed into objectives that have personal significance. In certain situations, what at first appears to be extrinsic incentive may eventually give way to intrinsic motivation.

- **Dual Insight:** People frequently feel both extrinsic and intrinsic motivation at the same time. For instance, a person who pursues a job for intrinsic (financial security) reasons could also sense intrinsic fulfillment in their employment.

- **Modifications in Drive:** Depending on how things are going personally or how circumstances change, the motivating emphasis may alter. It is possible for something that was first motivated by extrinsic causes to become intrinsically motivated, or vice versa.

Equanimity in Various Situations: While some activities—especially those in professional or educational settings—may be intrinsically motivating by nature, others may combine extrinsic and intrinsic motivators in order to provide a well-rounded approach.

Practical Implications and Considerations: Knowing the mechanics of intrinsic and extrinsic motivation is useful in a variety of settings, such as the workplace, education, and personal growth.

- **Learning Environments:** By designing learning environments that support intrinsic motivation through autonomy, mastery, and purpose and by rewarding accomplishments with suitable extrinsic rewards, educators can improve motivation in their students.

Motivation at Work: To maximize employee engagement and performance, effective leaders strike a balance between extrinsic motivators like recognition and prizes and intrinsic motivators like meaningful work and growth opportunities.

Individual Growth: People can strategically use both extrinsic and intrinsic motivators to achieve their aims. Sustaining motivation can be facilitated by realizing the harmony and balance between one's own interests and outside incentives.

In conclusion, the complexity of human behavior and performance is shaped by the interaction between intrinsic and extrinsic drive. Despite having different qualities, the two motivational sources are not exclusive. Understanding how these motives are interdependent enables a more complex comprehension of human behavior and offers guidance on how people can successfully channel these forces to promote success and fulfillment in different facets of existence.

4.2 Setting SMART Goals Aligned with Emotional Intelligence

A key component of both professional and personal development is goal-setting, and the efficacy and sustainability of these endeavors are increased when they are in line with emotional intelligence (EI). Setting goals is facilitated by the SMART criteria, which stand for Specific, Measurable, Achievable, Relevant, and Time-bound. SMART goals become an effective tool for relationship management, personal development, and general well-being when they are combined with the concepts of emotional intelligence.

Details:

Specificity in the context of emotional intelligence refers to precisely articulating the intended emotional result of skill development. A specific aim would be to "actively listen to colleagues during team meetings and respond empathetically to their ideas," as opposed to general ones like "improve communication skills." Because of its clarity, it offers a defined objective, which facilitates progress monitoring and helps define success.

Achievable:

For emotional intelligence goals to be successful, progress must be measured. A quantifiable objective might be, "Practice 10 minutes of mindfulness meditation daily to decrease stress levels," as opposed to a general one like "reduce stress." Measurable objectives enable people to monitor their progress, acknowledge minor successes, and make necessary corrections.

Achievable:

Achievable goals guarantee that they are reasonable and attainable. In terms of emotional intelligence, this could entail identifying one's own advantages and shortcomings. Achievable objectives can include, for example, "offer constructive feedback to team members in a positive manner during weekly meetings," taking into consideration the context of the interactions and the individual's communication style.

Pertinent:

Aligning emotional intelligence goals with more general personal or professional goals makes them relevant. One goal that may be appropriate would be to "cultivate a collaborative team culture by recognizing and appreciating individual contributions regularly" if the overall objective is to improve leadership skills. This purpose is in line with the more general goals of team dynamics and successful leadership.

Time-bound: Time-bound objectives have a deadline for completion, which gives them structure and a sense of urgency. A time-bound objective might be something like "finish a 4-week emotional intelligence training program and apply the learning in team interactions by the end of the month," as opposed to a general one like "improve emotional intelligence." This time restriction improves dedication and focus.

Integrated Emotional Intelligence:

1. Aims for Self-Awareness:

0 Particular:* Become more self-aware by recognizing and identifying your own triggers.

○ *Measurable:* Journal every day to document thoughts and feelings.

○ *Achievable:* Begin with a particular facet of self-awareness, like identifying feelings under duress.

Pertinent: Comply with the objective of cultivating affective self-awareness to enhance decision-making.

○ *Time-bound:* Establish a deadline of one month to finish a self-evaluation and find trends.

2. **Self-Regulation Objectives:** - *Details:* Establish self-control by pausing before reacting to difficult circumstances.

▪ Measurable:* Keep track of the occasions when the pause was effectively applied and record the resulting emotional effects.

0 *Achievable:* Start with low-stakes scenarios and progressively apply self-control in more difficult settings.

Pertinent: Align with the overarching objective of fostering emotional fortitude and proficient dispute resolution.

Time-bound: Over the course of the following two weeks, regularly apply the pause strategy.

3. **Empathy Objectives:** - *Detailed:* Develop empathy by actively hearing colleagues out without passing judgment.

▪ Measurable:* Document the occurrences of active listening and the effects on relationships.

0 *Achievable:* Begin with brief discussions and work your way up to longer, more involved ones.

Pertinent: Align with the objective of fostering a cooperative work atmosphere and wholesome connections.

○ *Time-bound:* Over the course of the following month, regularly incorporate active listening into team meetings.

4. **Social Skills Objectives:** - *Details:* Boost social skills by giving constructive criticism in a kind way.

■ Measurable:* Monitor when feedback is given and evaluate the team's reaction.

0 *Achievable:* Start with brief, frequent feedback sessions and work your way up to longer, more thorough assessments.

Pertinent: Comply with the objective of enhancing correspondence and cultivating a constructive team environment.

○ *Time-bound:* Within the next two weeks, have a feedback session with every team member.

5. **Drive and Objective Establishing Objectives:

■ Specific:* Boost motivation by establishing and accomplishing targeted emotional intelligence objectives.

■ Measurable:* Establish checkpoints for every objective and assess advancement frequently.

Achievable: Make sure the objectives are doable and attainable through a step-by-step breakdown.

0 *Relevant:* Use emotional intelligence to relate to the main goal of professional and personal development.

○ *Time-bound:* Set deadlines for each goal's completion and perform a thorough review in three months.

Advantages of Matching Emotional Intelligence with Goals:

1. **Enhanced Self-Awareness:** Emotionally intelligent SMART objectives help people become more self-aware by helping them recognize their feelings, assets, and opportunities for growth.
2. **Enhanced Interpersonal Relationships:** Empathy, attentive listening, and constructive communication are goals that lead to better interpersonal relationships in both the personal and professional spheres.
3. **Effective Conflict Resolution:** Increasing social and self-control

SMART goals provide people the skills they need to resolve disputes in a positive way.

1. **Professional Growth:** Goals that are in line with emotional intelligence will help you advance in your career because employers highly respect effective leadership and interpersonal abilities.
2. **Overall Well-Being:** Reaching emotional intelligence objectives enhances resilience, overall well-being, and a sense of fulfillment.

In summary, SMART goals that incorporate emotional intelligence concepts produce a comprehensive framework for both professional and personal growth. Through the establishment of clear, quantifiable, attainable, pertinent, and time-bound goals, people can systematically improve their emotional intelligence, leading to positive transformation and development in a variety of areas of their lives.

4.3 Overcoming Procrastination and Cultivating Persistence

Delaying or postponing chores is a frequent difficulty that many people encounter in several spheres of their lives. This is known as procrastination. Gaining the ability to overcome procrastination and develop persistence is crucial for improving productivity as well as general wellbeing and personal development. This section examines the causes of procrastination, methods for overcoming it, and how tenacity develops into a critical success factor.

Comprehending Delayed Responses:

The complicated phenomena of procrastination is impacted by a number of variables, such as situational, psychological, and emotional aspects. It usually entails staying away from activities that are thought to be difficult, unpleasant, or anxious-inducing. Delaying work can provide procrastinators with a little sensation of relaxation, but it can also result in higher stress levels, decreased self-esteem, and lost possibilities for personal development.

Procrastination-Inducing Factors:

1. **Insufficient Drive:** People tend to put off jobs that don't have a clear goal or intrinsic drive, especially if the rewards aren't visible right away.
2. **dread of Failure:** Procrastination is a coping mechanism for the dread of maybe failing to live up to one's own or other people's expectations.
3. The Aim for Perfection: It can be paralyzing to aim for perfection. Tasks may be put off by procrastinators because they are afraid they won't match their very high expectations.
4. **Complexity of Task:** Overly difficult or unclear chores can be intimidating, which makes people put them off beginning or finishing.
5. **Ineffective Time Management:** People who struggle to prioritize and manage their time well tend to put off doing things because they feel overburdened by the amount of work they have to do.

Tips for Beating Procrastination:

1. **Divide jobs into Smaller Steps:** - Larger jobs become less daunting when they are divided into smaller, more doable steps. Reaching these tiny milestones gives you a sense of advancement and success.
2. **Establish Specific and Doable Objectives:** - Clarity and focus are produced by setting SMART (specific, measurable, achievable, relevant, and time-bound) goals. Setting and sticking to clear goals helps you stay on track and minimizes procrastination.
3. **Create Intrinsic Motivation** - Intrinsic motivation is increased when tasks are linked to long-term objectives and personal values. Comprehending the importance of a task

might enhance its appeal and lessen the inclination to put it off.

4. **Control Perfectionism:** - It's important to identify and confront perfectionistic inclinations. Overcoming the fear of imperfection is made easier by realizing that projects don't have to be perfect and that making mistakes is a necessary part of learning.

5. **Make an Organized Timetable:** - Creating a well-organized daily or weekly agenda facilitates efficient time management. Procrastination is less likely when jobs are assigned precise time periods and deadlines are met.

6. **Apply Time-Blocking Techniques:** - Time blocking entails allocating particular time blocks to specific tasks. By reducing distractions and fostering attention, this method makes it simpler to overcome procrastination.

7. **Visualize Success:** - Encouraging positive thinking and motivation is fostered by visualizing successful task completion. The bad feelings that cause procrastination can be offset by thinking about the benefits of finishing a task.

8. **Engage in Self-Compassion Exercises:** Self-compassion cultivation entails being compassionate and understanding to oneself. Recognizing that everyone experiences difficulties and failures aids in overcoming the procrastination-inducing dread of failing.

9. **Establish Accountability:** - Accountability is created when goals are shared with friends, mentors, or coworkers. The knowledge that another person is aware of one's goals might serve as inspiration to maintain focus.

10. **Apply the Two-Minute Rule:** - According to the two-minute rule, any work that takes two minutes or less should be finished right away. This reduces the amount of little jobs that build up and cause procrastination.

Building Sturdiness:

The capacity to keep going for objectives in the face of difficulties, failures, and roadblocks is known as persistence. It is a crucial quality shared by exceptional performers and is intimately related to resilience. Developing a mindset that sees obstacles as chances for improvement and perceives failures as transient impediments rather than insurmountable hurdles is essential to cultivating persistence.

Methods for Fostering Persistence:

1. **Establish Long-Term Objectives:** - Setting meaningful, attainable long-term goals gives one direction and purpose. Long-term objectives serve as motivation, urging people to keep going in the face of immediate difficulties.

2. **Focus on the Process:** - Persistence is increased when the emphasis is shifted from merely outcome-oriented goals to the process of learning and improvement. A resilient mindset is fostered by accepting the path.

3. **Take A Lesson from Failures:** - Being persistent means that you see setbacks as learning opportunities rather than failures. Sustaining success involves evaluating failures, drawing conclusions, and modifying tactics.

4. **Cultivate a Growth mentality:** – Having a growth mentality is thinking that intelligence and skill can be acquired with commitment and work. This way of thinking encourages perseverance and resilience in the face of difficulties.

5. **Celebrate Small Wins:** - Giving credit to and acknowledging little victories along the road gives reinforcement that is constructive. This acknowledgement of efforts encourages perseverance by showcasing advancements and successes.

6. **Surround Yourself with Support:** - Having a network of friends, mentors, and coworkers at your side can be a source of encouragement when things become tough. Persistence might

be strengthened by others' counsel and experiences that are shared.

7. **Maintain Flexibility:** - Adaptability is necessary to cultivate tenacity. Having an adaptable mindset and being prepared to change tactics as needed are key components of long-term success.

8. **Remain Inspired:** – Retaining motivation can be achieved by taking cues from successful people, role models, or own ideals. In difficult times, inspiration serves as a motivator.

9. **Build Resilience:** Persistence and resilience are intimately related. Resilience is the capacity to overcome hardship. People that are resilient see obstacles as opportunities and show that they have what it takes to keep going when things get tough.

10. **Practice Self-Discipline:** - Consistently making decisions that are in line with long-term objectives is a necessary part of developing self-discipline. By guaranteeing steady effort throughout time, self-discipline practices strengthen perseverance.

Combining Overcoming Procrastination with Developing Perseverance:

1. **Identify Procrastination Triggers:** - By identifying particular circumstances or feelings that cause procrastination, people can put solutions into place to stop this habit.

2. **Set Proactive Goals:** - Proactive goal setting entails foreseeing possible obstacles and creating plans to overcome them. By being proactive, procrastination is less likely to occur.

3. **Establish Milestones:** - Dividing more ambitious objectives into more manageable benchmarks offers chances to

acknowledge accomplishments and motivate perseverance.

4. **Embrace a Growth Mindset:** - Developing a growth mindset makes it easier for people to overcome obstacles, see failures as teaching opportunities, and develop a resilient and tenacious mindset.

...

1. **Regularly Review Progress:** - Individuals can evaluate their journey, make required adjustments, and maintain motivation by periodically examining their progress toward goals.

2. **Reward Persistence:** - Positive behavior is reinforced when a system of rewards is put in place for consistent effort. Incentives can be extrinsic—like rewarding oneself for reaching a goal—or intrinsic—like self-praise.

3. **Ask for input:** - Asking for input from peers or mentors helps people keep on track and gives insightful information about areas that need work.

4. **Practice Self-Reflection:** - People who regularly engage in self-reflection are able to examine the causes of their procrastination and evaluate their level of perseverance in general. Sincere introspection is a potent instrument for personal development.

Advantages of Developing Persistence and Overcoming Procrastination:

1. **Enhanced Productivity:** Since activities are tackled and finished on time, overcoming procrastination and cultivating determination lead to enhanced productivity.

2. **Improved Welfare:** Procrastination frequently results in tension and nervousness. Improving mental and emotional health is a result of breaking this tendency and developing

perseverance.

3. **Higher Goal Achievement:** People who strive for their objectives with perseverance are more likely to succeed in doing so. Pursuing goals consistently is ensured by overcoming procrastination.

4. **Enhanced Self-Efficaciousness:** Overcoming procrastination and persevering through difficulties improves self-efficacy, or the conviction that one can accomplish their goals. Consequently, this fosters a cheerful outlook.

5. **Increased Adaptability:** Resilience and persistence cultivation go hand in hand. People who persevere in the face of adversity build resilience, which enables them to overcome obstacles with more resiliency.

6. **Good Effect on Interactions:** Relationships are positively impacted by the capacity to overcome procrastination and persevere in both personal and professional endeavors. It promotes dependability, trust, and a feeling of accomplishment among everybody.

In summary, developing tenacity and conquering procrastination simultaneously can have a profoundly positive impact on one's personal and professional growth. People can develop a persistent attitude that drives them toward achievement, resilience, and general well-being by comprehending the underlying causes of procrastination and putting solutions in place to solve them.

4.4 Techniques for Maintaining Motivation

The engine that propels goal pursuit and accomplishment is motivation. But maintaining motivation over time can be difficult since people run into roadblocks, disappointments, and diversions. Many strategies can be used to develop a constant and durable motivating mindset. This section examines practical methods for encouraging perseverance, boosting overall goal achievement, and sustaining motivation in the face of difficulties.

1. **Establish Specific and Valuable Objectives:** A feeling of purpose and direction can be obtained by setting meaningful and explicit goals. Having well-defined goals acts as a road map, pointing people in the direction of their desired outcomes. Goal specificity increases motivation and focus maintenance.

2. **Divide Objectives Into More Manageable Tasks:** The road to success becomes more accessible when more ambitious objectives are divided into smaller, more doable activities. When these tiny chores are finished, a sense of achievement is felt, which boosts drive and builds momentum.

3. **Establish a Graphical Representation:** - Creating a written list or vision board as a visual aid for your goals will help you stay motivated. People who regularly check this visual reminder are better able to connect with their goals and stay focused on the intended results.

4. **Create a Schedule:** - Creating a routine offers consistency and organization. Routines establish habits, and habits reduce the amount of conscious effort needed to perform an activity. By incorporating goal-related activities into everyday life, this can assist people in maintaining their motivation.

5. **Appreciate Little Wins:** - Motivation is strengthened by acknowledging and appreciating little victories along the road. Acknowledging progress—even small ones—creates a positive feedback loop that motivates people to keep working hard.

6. **Look for Natural Motivators:** - Finding intrinsic motivators—such as one's own values, passions, or sense of purpose—helps people feel profoundly connected to their objectives. Motivators that come from within, originating from wants, are more enduring than those that come from outside sources.

7. **Adopt a Growth Mentality**: Having a growth mindset entails seeing obstacles as chances for development and learning. People who have a growth mentality view setbacks as stepping stones toward improvement, which makes them more resilient and driven to conquer challenges.

8. **Look for Social Assistance:** - A support network is created when objectives are shared with friends, family, or coworkers. Sustained motivation is facilitated by other people's accountability, positive reinforcement, and shared experiences. A network of allies can provide direction when things go tough.

9. **Apply Visualization Techniques:** - Visualization is the process of imagining oneself accomplishing objectives in one's mind. Through the use of visualization, this strategy makes people feel more achievable and motivated towards achieving their goals.

10. **Set Realistic Expectations:** – Setting reasonable expectations helps to avoid the demoralizing impact of unfulfilled expectations. By ensuring that people set realistic goals, realism reduces the possibility of disappointment and promotes long-term motivation.

11. **Create a Reward Structure:** - Setting up a reward system

gives people motivation to reach goals. Incentives might be extrinsic—like treating oneself to a little celebration—or intrinsic—like personal fulfillment. Positive behavior is rewarded by this.

12. **Remain Adaptable:** - Remaining flexible in the face of shifting conditions is essential to sustaining drive. Staying adaptable and making appropriate adjustments to goals or techniques can help people maintain motivation in ever-changing circumstances.

13. **Track Your Progress:** - People can evaluate their journey by tracking their progress toward goals on a regular basis. Sustaining motivation is facilitated by keeping track of accomplishments, pinpointing problem areas, and making the required corrections.

14. **Concentrate on the Why:** - Motivation is strengthened by getting back in touch with the fundamental causes or "why" of objectives. Comprehending the rationale and importance of pursuing particular goals aids individuals in maintaining their commitment, especially in the face of obstacles.

15. **Foster an Upbeat Attitude:** - Sustaining resilience and optimism are essential components of a positive mentality. Self-doubt and discouragement can be combated by positive thinking, which cultivates a driven perspective for the path ahead.

Rotate your activities: **16. Boredom and monotony can be avoided with variety. Changing around a goal's components or adding a variety of activities that are connected to it will keep motivation high and interest levels sustained throughout time.

1. **Examine Past Accomplishments:** - Examining previous accomplishments, regardless of size, provides a reminder of one's potential. A positive self-image is reinforced by this

reflection, which also increases enthusiasm to take on new objectives.

2. **Establish Reasonable Timeframes:** – Setting reasonable deadlines for achieving objectives helps shield you from disappointment when your expectations aren't fulfilled. Timelines that are realistic take into consideration the intricacies of the trip, encouraging perseverance and patience.

3. **Get Rid of or Control Distractions:** - To stay motivated and focused, it's critical to recognize and control distractions. Maintaining focus on objectives requires minimizing distractions and establishing a favorable environment.

4. **Take Part in Ongoing Education:** - Developing an attitude of perpetual learning encourages motivation. The pursuit of novel insights, abilities, and encounters invigorates the voyage and bolsters individual and occupational growth.

The advantages of staying motivated

1. **Increased Productivity:** - People who are consistently motivated to work toward their goals and overcome obstacles are more productive than others.

2. **Improved Well-Being:** - People who are motivated frequently report having better mental and emotional health. A sense of fulfillment and purpose is fostered by pursuing meaningful goals.

3. **Increased Sturdiness:** - A motivated mindset is closely tied to resilience. Individuals who maintain motivation are better equipped to bounce back from setbacks and persevere through difficulties.

4. **Positive Impact on Relationships:** - Motivated individuals often bring a positive and proactive attitude to their relationships. This can foster collaboration, support, and shared success within social networks.

5. **Continuous Personal Growth:** - Maintaining motivation promotes continuous personal growth. Individuals who stay motivated seek new challenges, acquire new skills, and embrace opportunities for self-improvement.

6. **Increased Goal Attainment:** - Sustained motivation significantly increases the likelihood of goal attainment. Consistent effort, focus, and adaptability contribute to successful outcomes.

7. **Strengthened Self-Confidence:** - Achieving goals through sustained motivation boosts self-confidence. Successes, even small ones, contribute to a positive self-image and a belief in one's capabilities.

8. **Enhanced Adaptability:** - Motivated individuals are more adaptable in the face of change. They approach challenges with a proactive mindset, seeking solutions and maintaining flexibility.

In short, the techniques for maintaining motivation are diverse and can be tailored to individual preferences and circumstances. Employing a combination of these strategies fosters a resilient and sustained motivational mindset, ensuring that individuals stay committed to their goals, overcome challenges, and experience continuous growth and success.

4.5 Visualizing Success and Motivational Techniques

Mental imaging, often known as visualization, is a potent technique that entails forming clear, vivid mental images of desired results. When paired with additional motivational strategies, it becomes an effective tool for improving output, building self-assurance, and upholding an optimistic outlook. The idea of picturing success is examined in this section, along with a number of motivational strategies people might use to spur action and accomplish their objectives.

1. Envisioning Achievement:

Explanation:

The process of creating a mental picture or scenario—often with sensory details—to mimic an experience or intended result is known as visualization. To visualize success, one must mentally practice reaching their objectives, envision the trip, and conjure up the happy feelings that come with accomplishment.

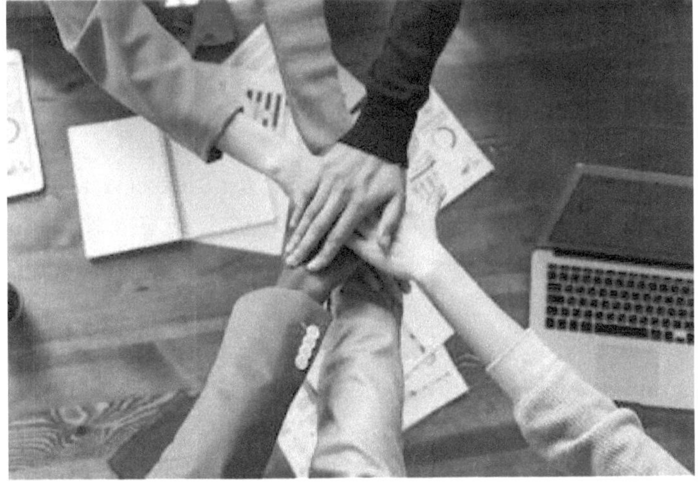

How Success Is Visualized:

Similar neural pathways in the brain are activated when people visualize achievement as opposed to when they actually experience it. This mental practice helps people get more comfortable with the intended result, lessens their fear of the unknown, and increases their confidence that achievement is possible.

Important Elements of Visualization:

1. **Emotional Picture:** Visualization works better when detailed, sensory-rich mental images are created. Using all of the senses—touch, sound, vision, and emotion—improves the realism of the imagined scene.

2. **Happy Feelings:** When pleasant feelings, like happiness, pride, or contentment, are associated with the visualization, its effect increases. The technique's motivational element is strengthened when one experiences the feelings linked to achievement.

3. **Reiteration:** Re-visiting and repeating the visualization on a regular basis strengthens its impact. Maintaining consistency in visualizing aids in ingraining the intended result into the subconscious, impacting attitudes and actions.

Visualization Applications:

1. **Achievement of Goal:** People can better connect their thoughts and behaviors with their goals by visualizing success. It gives a mental road map for the actions required to succeed, boosting drive and dedication.

2. **Improving Performance:** Visualization is a common tool used by professionals, artists, and athletes to improve performance. Visualizing a faultless performance or prosperous result can boost self-assurance and concentration.

3. **De-stressing:** Stress management can benefit greatly from the use of visualization. Reducing anxiety and fostering a sense of

control can be achieved by visualizing a peaceful and effective end to a difficult circumstance.

4. **Confidence-Building:** Creating successful situations in your mind's eye helps you become more confident. The idea that people are capable of overcoming challenges and realizing their goals is strengthened by the constructive mental rehearsal.

5. **Developing an Upbeat Attitude:** By concentrating on what can be accomplished rather than lingering on potential obstacles, visualization promotes a positive mindset. This upbeat viewpoint may influence how you solve problems and make decisions.

2. Strategies for Motivation:

**Strategies and procedures intended to stimulate and maintain motivation are known as motivational techniques. These methods, when paired with visualization, provide a thorough strategy for sustaining motivation and zeal. Here are a few successful motivational strategies: **

a. **Establishing Goals:** - Setting attainable objectives offers a motivational road map. Establishing goals that are precise, quantifiable, and time-bound gives one direction and purpose. Goal-setting and visualization work together to enhance motivation by having the latter idea of goal accomplishment come to mind.

b. **Encouragement Phrases:** - Positive affirmations are declarations that support optimistic attitudes and beliefs. Repeating affirmations on a daily basis helps modify mental patterns and cultivate a positive outlook. When visualization and positive affirmations are combined, the effects are enhanced since the intended results are reinforced in both words and pictures.

c. **Partners in Accountability:** - An accountability partner, such as a friend, mentor, or coworker, establishes a network of support. The sense of accountability and motivation is increased when goals and accomplishments are shared with others. Talking with an accountability partner about and reaffirming the common vision helps improve visualization.

d. **Effective Time Management:** - Managing your time well is a motivational strategy that lessens overload. Organizing work into digestible chunks and setting aside time for each one helps you feel like you're making progress. Motivation can be increased by using visualization to picture tasks being successfully completed within allotted time constraints.

e. **Inspirational Media:** - Getting inspiration from outside sources comes from watching movies, reading books, or listening to podcasts. Narratives of triumph, resiliency, and conquering obstacles can serve as a source of inspiration and enhance the intrinsic drive developed via visualization.

f. **Encouragement in the Workplace:** - Sustaining enthusiasm is facilitated by surrounding oneself with encouraging and positive people. An environment that is beneficial to sustaining drive and attention includes relationships that are supportive, an uncluttered workspace, and an upbeat vibe. Visualization complements this method by allowing one to envision achievement in the context of a favorable setting.

g. **Reflective activities:** - Journaling and mindfulness are two examples of reflective activities that help with self-awareness and motivation. Consistently contemplating on one's achievements, difficulties, and personal development strengthens one's dedication to their objectives. By seeing potential achievements and opportunities for development, visualization can be included into reflective activities.

h. **Reward Systems:** - Setting up a reward system encourages reaching objectives. Incentives boost motivation, whether they are extrinsic (material rewards) or intrinsic (personal fulfillment). By picturing the benefits of achieving a goal successfully, visualization can be utilized to generate strong motivation.

Advantages of Using Motivational Techniques and Visualizing Success:

1. **Enhanced Focus:** - Focus is improved by visualizing success since it helps to form an accurate mental picture of the intended result. Motivational tactics support this concentration by offering methods for keeping goals in the forefront of one's mind.

2. **Increased Confidence:** - By mentally practicing success, visualization increases confidence. When used in conjunction with other motivating strategies like goal-setting and positive affirmations, people grow to have a strong sense of self-worth.

3. **Sustained Motivation:** - A strong force for sustained motivation is produced by the interaction of motivational strategies and visualization. Practice on a regular basis strengthens the will to succeed in spite of obstacles.

4. **Enhanced Resilience:** Motivational approaches can build resilience, and visualization helps cultivate a positive mindset. When combined, they provide people the mental strength to push over obstacles and keep going after their goals.

5. **Goal Attainment:** - The probability of achieving a goal is greatly increased when motivational and visual aids are used together. People are inspired to consistently go toward their objectives, bringing their ideas into reality.

6. **Positive Mindset:** - Motivational and visualization methods both help to

developing an optimistic outlook. This upbeat perspective affects beliefs, actions, and general wellbeing.

In conclusion, motivating strategies combined with success visualization produce a potent combination that promotes both professional and personal growth. People can motivate themselves to take action, stay enthusiastic, and accomplish their goals by combining goal-setting, positive affirmations, vivid mental imagery, and other motivational techniques. By addressing both the cognitive and emotional aspects of motivation, this all-encompassing strategy offers a thorough framework for achievement.

Chapter 5: Empathy and Social Skills

5.1 Enhancing Empathetic Understanding

An essential component of interpersonal relationships and productive communication is empathy, or the capacity to recognize and experience another person's emotions. Improving empathy comprehension requires more than just acknowledging others' feelings and viewpoints; it calls for a thoughtful and caring interaction with them. The significance of empathy, the elements of empathetic understanding, and useful techniques to improve this vital interpersonal ability are all covered in this section.

1. Realizing the Value of Empathy:

Empathy serves as a link between people, promoting mutual respect, comprehension, and deep connections. In many facets of life, including interpersonal relationships, the job, and social interactions, empathy is essential to fostering a positive and cooperative atmosphere. It enables people to relate to one another's experiences, encouraging empathy, teamwork, and a sense of our common humanity.

Important Facets of Empathy:

1. **Cognitive Empathy:** entails comprehending the viewpoint, feelings, and thoughts of another individual. It calls for attentive attention, an open mind, and the capacity to understand many points of view.

2. **Emotional Empathy:** Consists of sharing and relating to other people's feelings. This means feeling some of the same emotions as the other person as well as comprehending their sentiments intellectually.

3. **Compassionate Empathy:** Encourages a desire to lessen the pain or difficulties that others are facing, taking empathy a step further. It entails having a sincere care for other people's welfare and being prepared to provide assistance.

1. **Elements of Empathy Perception:**

a. **Paying Attention:** - Empathic comprehension is based on the fundamental skill of active listening. It entails paying close attention to and understanding all that someone is saying, both out loud and nonverbally. People show their dedication to understanding others by paying close attention, seeking clarification, and paraphrasing.

b. Viewpoint Interpretation:

The capacity to perceive a situation from the perspective of another person is known as perspective-taking. It necessitates moving beyond one's own perspective and taking the other person's context, feelings, and thoughts into account.

a. **Emotional Regulation:** - Effective emotional regulation is a prerequisite for empathic comprehension. To foster a secure and encouraging environment where people feel free to express themselves, it is necessary to be conscious of one's own emotional reactions and to control them appropriately.

b. **Non-Verbal Communication:** - A person's body language, tone of voice, and facial expressions all provide a plethora of information about their emotional condition. Gaining awareness of these indicators improves empathy comprehension by offering context outside of spoken words.

c. **Reflective reactions:** - Reflective reactions entail reflecting and approving the feelings that people convey. Sayings like "I can understand why that would be challenging" or "It sounds like you're feeling..." in response shows empathy and validates the recognition of other people's feelings.

d. **Empathetic Questioning:** - Empathetic understanding is fostered by open-ended questions that encourage people to talk more about their experiences. Asking thoughtful questions demonstrates a sincere desire to comprehend the subtleties of other people's thoughts and emotions.

e. **Cultural Competence:** - Acknowledging and honoring a variety of cultural origins, experiences, and beliefs is a component of cultural competence. By recognizing the influence of cultural elements on people's feelings and viewpoints, cultural competence improves empathy comprehension.

3. Useful Techniques to Improve Empathic Perception:

a. **Engage in Mindful Listening**: Being totally present and paying close attention to the speaker are two aspects of mindful listening. Reduce distractions as much as possible, make eye contact, and avoid interjecting. A greater comprehension of the speaker's motivations and feelings is facilitated by this concentrated attention.

b. **Foster Curiosity:** - Fostering curiosity about the experiences of others promotes a sincere interest in their viewpoints. Encourage others to talk more about their feelings, ideas, and experiences by posing open-ended inquiries.

c. **Study Empathy-Related Literature:** - Reading books that examine interpersonal connections, emotional intelligence, and empathy can offer insightful viewpoints. Books, articles, and research studies can help people understand empathy better and provide useful advice on how to improve it.

d. **Attend Training or seminars on Empathy:** - Taking part in training or seminars on empathy offers organized learning opportunities. These classes frequently involve role-playing, interactive exercises, and conversations to assist people improve their capacity for sympathetic comprehension.

e. **Take Part in Reflective Practices:** - People can evaluate their sympathetic reactions by regularly reflecting on their encounters with others. Think about the ways in which one's personal experiences and prejudices may color perceptions and endeavor to develop a more impartial and open-minded viewpoint.

f. **Seek Diverse Perspectives:** - Make a conscious effort to be exposed to a variety of viewpoints and experiences. Interacting with people from diverse origins, cultures, and lifestyles enhances comprehension and fosters a compassionate consciousness of a range of feelings and difficulties.

g. **Journaling with Empathy:** - Writing in an empathic notebook is thinking back on everyday encounters and highlighting situations when sympathetic understanding was applied well or might be strengthened. This introspective exercise promotes ongoing development and increases self-awareness.

h. **Volunteer or Take Part in Service Activities:** - Participating in volunteer work or service projects offers opportunity to put empathy into practice. Engaging with people who are struggling or making a positive contribution to the community's well-being cultivates empathy and a caring outlook.

Advantages of Improving Empathy Recognition:

1. **Enhanced Connections:** - Better understanding of empathy fosters deeper, more meaningful connections. When others recognize and understand their emotions, people feel appreciated and supported.

2. **Effective Communication:** - By encouraging clarity and mutual understanding, sympathetic understanding supports effective communication. It lessens miscommunication and conflict, promoting an atmosphere of open communication.

3. **Enhanced Collaboration and Trust:** - Empathy understanding is the cornerstone upon which trust is based. People build trust when they feel heard and understood, which promotes more productive collaboration in both personal and professional contexts.

Conflict Settlement

:** - Constructive conflict resolution relies heavily on empathy. Comprehending the feelings and viewpoints of all stakeholders involved facilitates more sophisticated and cooperative problem-solving.

1. **Enhanced Emotional Intelligence:** - A fundamental aspect of emotional intelligence is the capacity for empathy. Gaining proficiency in this area improves emotional intelligence generally, which benefits both personal and professional success.

2. **Good Impact on Well-Being:** - Empathy has a beneficial impact on well-being for both the giver and the recipient. Providing sympathetic understanding fosters a supportive atmosphere that boosts emotional fortitude and a sense of community.

3. **Cultural Competence:** - Developing empathy is a necessary component of cultural competence. Harmony in multicultural environments is promoted by inclusive attitudes and actions that are fostered by understanding and valuing other perspectives.

To sum up, developing empathetic understanding is a life-changing process that fosters personal development, stronger bonds with others, and beneficial effects on society.

People who actively practice empathy build relationships that cut over divides and promote a world that is kinder and more understanding.

5.2 Effective Communication Strategies

Successful interactions in any setting—personal, professional, or larger society contexts—are based on effective communication. It entails communicating ideas clearly, paying attention when others are speaking, and appreciating their viewpoints. This section explores the significance of good communication, essential elements of communication plans, and useful methods to improve communication abilities.

1. Realizing the Value of Skillful Communication:

Mutual understanding, teamwork, and good relationships all depend on effective communication. It involves more than just talking to someone; it is listening intently, using both verbal and nonverbal clues, and delivering messages that will be understood by the target audience. Effective communication builds emotional attachments and settles disputes in interpersonal relationships; in work environments, it promotes collaboration, creativity, and successful project outputs.

Important Elements of Good Communication:

1. **Unambiguity:** Effective communication guarantees that the recipient will understand the intended message with ease. It entails clearly expressing ideas and thoughts while avoiding ambiguity or uncertainty.

2. Paying Attention Actively: A key element of good communication is active listening. It entails paying close attention to the speaker, comprehending what they have to say, and intelligently answering. A sensation of being heard and respected is fostered by active listening.

3. **Compassion:** In order to communicate with empathy, one must be aware of and sensitive to the feelings and viewpoints of others. It establishes a rapport by exhibiting a sincere concern for the communicator's well.

4. **Non-Verbal Communication:** Non-verbal clues that convey additional layers of meaning include body language, tone of voice, and facial expressions. Using nonverbal cues and being aware of them increases the overall impact of messages.

5. **Reactions:** A crucial component of good communication is constructive criticism. It guarantees that the intended message is understood, encourages progress, and offers insightful information.

1. **Doable Techniques for Powerful Communication:**

a. **Clear Articulation:** Effective communication is predicated on the ability to articulate ideas and concepts in a clear and concise manner. A clear message can be achieved by avoiding jargon, speaking succinctly, and rationally arranging the material.

b. **Customizing the Message:** - Relevance and engagement are ensured by customizing the message to the audience. When structuring communication to maximize understanding, take the recipient's preferences, knowledge level, and background into consideration.

c. **Active Listening Techniques:** - Active listening entails paying close attention to what is being said, paraphrasing to make sure you understand, and reacting correctly. This tactic shows respect for the speaker and improves understanding.

d. **Empathetic Communication:** – Empathy is acknowledging and approving other people's feelings. A helpful and understanding environment is promoted when communication uses empathic language and expressions.

e. **Awareness of Nonverbal Cues:** Understanding nonverbal clues improves communication. To stay true to the intended message and project sincerity, keep your eyes open, adjust your tone, and maintain eye contact.

f. **Use of Visual Aids:** - Slides, graphs, and charts are examples of visual aids that can enhance spoken communication. Visual aids support various learning styles and aid in the clarification of difficult knowledge.

Select the Correct Channels: **g. It's important to choose the appropriate communication medium. Whether via email, video calls, or in-person interactions, selecting the best channel guarantees efficient message delivery.

a. **Timely and Consistent Communication:** - Communication that is timely and consistent fosters confidence. Transparency is promoted and misunderstandings are avoided by informing stakeholders and providing regular updates.

b. **Adaptability:** - Adapting to the situation and audience requirements is part of being flexible in communication.

Being adaptable guarantees that the message is understood clearly and favorably.

c. **Constructive Feedback:** - Specific, constructive, and actionable feedback is a key component of good communication. It fortifies professional connections, encourages progress, and makes expectations clear.

d. **Skills for Resolving Conflicts:** - Resolving conflicts is an essential component of good communication. A cooperative and positive atmosphere is fostered by the development of conflict resolution, conflict resolution, and conflict resolution abilities.

e. **Cultural Sensitivity:** - Recognizing and honoring various cultural norms and communication styles is a component of cultural sensitivity. Understanding is facilitated in multicultural environments when communication is modified to be inclusive and culturally sensitive.

f. **Mindful Communication:** - Mindful communication involves giving the conversation your whole attention and being in the moment. More meaningful conversation can be achieved by putting aside distractions, exercising patience, and paying close attention.

g. **Cooperation Among Teams:** - Collaboration in team environments depends on efficient communication. Team success is influenced by promoting open communication, active involvement, and a culture of trust.

Effective Communication's Benefits:

1. **Building Strong Relationships:** - Meaningful and strong relationships are fostered by effective communication on both a personal and professional level. Building trust and understanding requires open and honest communication.

2. **Increased Cooperation:** - Collaboration in professional

settings requires efficient communication to be successful. Effectively communicating teams are more likely to accomplish shared objectives and perform effectively on projects.

3. **dispute Resolution:** - One of the most important aspects of dispute resolution is effective communication. Finding common ground, addressing differences, and coming to mutually beneficial settlements are all facilitated by clear and sympathetic communication.

4. **Enhanced Productivity:** - Enhanced productivity is a result of clear communication. Work is completed more quickly when expectations, guidelines, and comments are conveyed clearly.

5. **Innovation and Creativity:** - The exchange of ideas and viewpoints is encouraged in a culture that values good communication. People become more innovative and creative as a result of feeling free to voice their opinions and participate in brainstorming sessions.

6. **Personal and Professional Development:** - Effective communication abilities support both personal and professional development. People with strong communication skills, active listening skills, and interpersonal engagement skills are more likely to succeed.

7. **Positive Work Environment:** - A positive work environment is facilitated by effective communication. People feel more acknowledged, appreciated, and understood, which boosts morale and creates an environment that is more successful and cooperative overall.

8. **Satisfied Customers:** - Effective communication is essential for client happiness in company and customer service. Transparent and prompt communication improves client satisfaction and fosters confidence.

To sum up, proficient communication is a complex ability that includes a range of approaches and elements. Learning, changing, and honing one's communication style to suit the requirements of various audiences and situations is a continuous process. People may improve their ability to communicate by putting clarity, active listening, empathy, and cultural sensitivity first. This will lead to stronger bonds, more productive teams, and overall success.

5.3 Conflict Resolution and Relationship Building

Human interactions will inevitably result in conflict since different viewpoints, interests, and values will always arise. In social, professional, and personal contexts, the ability to resolve conflicts amicably and foster positive connections are critical competencies. The importance of conflict resolution, the fundamentals of effective conflict resolution, and methods for establishing and preserving enduring relationships are all covered in this section.

1. Realizing the Importance of Resolving Conflicts:

When handled well, conflict can promote development, creativity, and closer bonds between people. The process of confronting and settling disagreements in a way that promotes mutual respect and collaboration is known as conflict resolution. Whether in the family, at work, or in the community, good conflict resolution is essential to preserving connections.

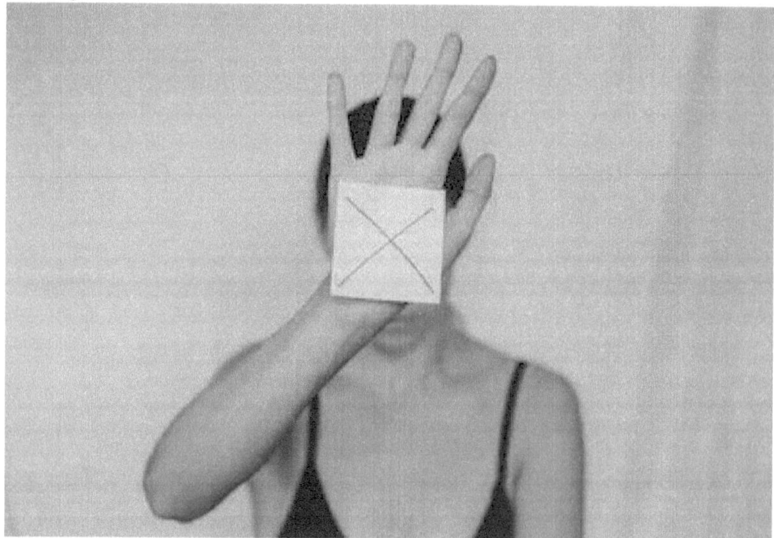

Principles Crucial to Effective Conflict Resolution:

1. **Open Communication:** - Honest and transparent communication is the cornerstone of resolving disputes. Establishing a secure environment in which all individuals can freely communicate their ideas and emotions promotes openness and comprehension.

2. **Active Listening:** - Prior to answering, active listening entails completely comprehending the viewpoints of others. It calls for tolerance, compassion, and a sincere desire to understand the fundamental worries of all sides.

3. **Empathy:** - An essential component of conflict resolution is empathy. Comprehending the feelings and intentions of others fosters empathy and lays the groundwork for resolving conflicts amicably.

4. **Collaboration:** - A fundamental idea is cooperative problem-solving. A collaborative approach looks for solutions that take into account the needs and interests of all parties engaged in the issue rather than seeing it as a win-lose situation.

5. **Respect:** - It is crucial to respect each person's autonomy and sense of dignity. It entails abstaining from insulting remarks, disparaging language, and rude conduct when resolving disputes.

1. **Techniques for Resolving Conflicts:**

a. **Determine the Root Cause:** - It's important to comprehend the underlying problems that are generating the dispute. Finding the underlying reason makes it easier to address the main issues rather than merely the symptomatology.

b. **Find a Common Ground:** - Establishing a common ground lays the groundwork for a resolution. Finding common interests or objectives facilitates communication and lays the groundwork for group problem-solving.

c. **Make Use of "I" Statements:** Using "I" phrases to communicate emotions and worries lessens defensiveness. For instance, framing sentences with "I feel" rather than "You always" emphasizes personal experiences.

d. **Seek Understanding:** - Make a conscious effort to comprehend other people's viewpoints. Paraphrasing, summarizing, and asking clarifying questions help to make sure that everyone feels understood and heard.

e. **Investigate Solutions Together:** - Working together to solve problems fosters a sense of dedication and ownership for the solutions. Promote ideation and group exploration of possibilities.

f. **Keep Your Cool and Show Respect:** - When resolving conflicts, emotional control is essential. Even when there are arguments, keeping your composure and manners will help to create a productive environment.

g. **Take Breaks When Needed:** - It can be helpful to take breaks if emotions get intense. Removing oneself from the present circumstance enables people to gather their thoughts and address the conflict from a more objective standpoint.

h. **Pay Attention to the Future:** - Focus on building a bright future rather than lamenting the past. Having a conversation on how to proceed and make adjustments keeps disagreements from spiraling out of control.

i. **Seek Mediation if Needed:** - When disputes don't seem to go away, it can be helpful to enlist the aid of an impartial mediator. Mediators assist parties in reaching mutually acceptable agreements by facilitating communication and directing conversations.

j. **Define Clear Agreements:** - It is crucial to define agreements and expectations that arise from resolving conflicts in a clear and concise manner. This avoids misconceptions and offers a foundation for subsequent conversations.

k. **Learn and Grow from Conflict:** - Conflict can be reframed as a chance for personal development. Personal and interpersonal development is facilitated by thinking back on the lessons learnt and using them in subsequent interactions.

3. Establishing and Preserving Powerful Bonds:

Building and sustaining healthy relationships requires proactive measures to foster understanding and connection in addition to dispute resolution. Building relationships can be facilitated by the following techniques, whether in personal or professional contexts:

a. **Proficiency in Communication:** - Building relationships is based on effective communication. Understanding and connection are cultivated via regular expression of thoughts, feelings, and expectations.

b. **Transparency and Trust:** - Trust-building calls for consistency and openness. Relationship trust is established via open communication, honesty, and dependability.

c. **Mutual Respect:** - It is imperative to show respect for the independence, beliefs, and limits of others. A respectful connection is fostered by treating others with dignity and taking the time to understand their viewpoints.

d. **Shared Values and Goals:** - A feeling of shared purpose is produced when values and goals are in line. Having similar goals for a relationship builds its basis, whether it be personal or professional.

e. **Quality Time:** - Relationships are strengthened when meaningful time is spent together. Spending quality time together fosters connection, whether through shared experiences, activities, or conversations.

f. **Strategies for Conflict Prevention:** - Preventing escalation of conflict by proactively addressing potential sources of conflict. Clearly defining expectations, being transparent in communication, and

Resolving issues when they come up helps to avoid conflicts.

a. **Empathy and Understanding:** - Relationships are improved by empathic understanding. An environment that is caring and supportive is produced when people take the time to comprehend the feelings, viewpoints, and needs of others.

b. **Celebration of Successes:** - Highlighting successes in the relationship strengthens good experiences no matter how big or small. A culture of gratitude and encouragement to one another is fostered by acknowledging accomplishments.

c. **Ongoing Education and Adjustment:** - People change over time, and relationships also change. Resilience and longevity in relationships are ensured by embracing ongoing learning and adaptability to the shifting dynamics of partnerships.

d. **Compromise and Flexibility:** - In partnerships, it's essential to be flexible and willing to make concessions. The key to a happy relationship is having an open mind and looking for solutions that satisfy the requirements of both sides.

e. **Offer Apologies and Forgiveness:** - Maintaining relationships requires offering forgiveness and offering an apology when needed. Sincere apologies, forgiveness, and acknowledging mistakes all help the relationship to mend and prosper.

Advantages of Relationship Building and Effective Conflict Resolution:

1. **Healthy Relationships:** - The growth of wholesome, gratifying relationships is facilitated by effective conflict

resolution and relationship building. People experience connection, understanding, and support.

2. **Enhanced Cooperation and Productivity:** - Effective conflict resolution improves teamwork and efficiency in work environments. Constructive conflict resolution makes teams more capable of achieving shared objectives.

3. **Emotional Well-Being:** - Emotional well-being is influenced by positive interactions. Mental and emotional wellness is enhanced when one feels appreciated, supported, and connected.

4. **Innovation and Creativity:** - A creative and innovative atmosphere is created by strong partnerships. People are at ease sharing their thoughts and working together to come up with original solutions.

5. **A Positive Culture Within the Organization:** - Good relationships and effective conflict resolution are two factors that support a positive corporate culture in the workplace. Overall job satisfaction and morale are raised in an environment of trust and cooperation.

6. **Resilience in Adversity:** - Effectively resolved conflicts strengthen relationships, making them more robust to hardship. Together, people overcome obstacles and come out stronger as a result.

7. **Personal Growth and Development:** - Constant learning and personal growth are necessary for conflict resolution and relationship building. People develop their capacity for emotional intelligence, effective communication, and flexibility.

To sum up, healthy relationships and interactions are woven together by the processes of relationship building and conflict resolution. People can create resilient connections that endure difficulties and advance both individual and societal well-being by actively fostering relationships, using good communication techniques, and approaching conflicts with a positive mentality.

5.4 Active Listening and Empathy in Conversations

In order to communicate effectively, one must actively listen to and comprehend others in addition to expressing oneself. Empathy and active listening are the cornerstones of meaningful and genuine communication. This section examines the value of empathy and active listening, as well as its essential elements and revolutionary effects on interpersonal communication.

Recognizing the Importance of Active Listening:

Communicating effectively requires more than just hearing what is being said; active listening entails giving the speaker your whole attention, paying attention to what they are saying, and showing that you genuinely want to know how they see things. Active listening is an effective strategy for establishing rapport, promoting understanding, and navigating challenging conversations in a world full of distractions and information overload.

1. **Important Elements of Active Listening:**
    1. **Giving Full Attention: -** The first step in active listening is to give the speaker all of your attention. A setting that is conducive to active listening is one that minimizes distractions, maintains eye contact, and communicates through body language that the speaker has one's full attention.
    2. **Paraphrasing and Summarizing: -** Offering an opportunity for clarification and demonstrating knowledge of the speaker's message through reflection and summarization. Rephrasing the speaker's words to make sure the listener understands the intended meaning is known as

paraphrasing.

3. **Asking Clarifying Questions:** - To show that you are committed to understanding, ask clarifying questions. Posing open-ended questions enables the speaker to go into more detail and provide more context and subtlety.

4. **Avoiding Interrupting:** - Interrupting can be interpreted as impolite and disturbs the flow of speech. Avoiding interruptions and giving the speaker time to finish speaking before answering are examples of active listening.

5. **Offering response:** - Giving verbal and nonverbal response indicates that the person being listened to is paying attention and taking the information in. A positive feedback loop is facilitated by confirming remarks, nodding, and demonstrating empathy with your face.

2. **Empathy's Place in Conversations:**

The capacity to comprehend and experience another person's emotions is known as empathy. Empathy in communication is more than just comprehending what is being said; it's about feeling the same feelings, opinions, and life experiences as the other person. Empathic communication improves the quality of relationships and fosters a sense of connection by establishing an environment that is affirming and helpful.

Important Elements of Empathic Communication:

1. **Recognizing Emotions:** - Understanding the speaker's conveyed emotions is the first step towards developing empathy. In order to ascertain the underlying emotions and experiences being expressed, this entails paying attention to both verbal and nonverbal clues.

2. **Expressing Understanding:** - Putting understanding into words by making sympathetic remarks indicates that the listener is aware of the speaker's feelings. Expressions like "That sounds challenging" or "I can imagine how that must feel" provide validation and empathy.

3. **Cognitive Empathy:** - This type of empathy entails comprehending the viewpoint and ideas of the speaker. Even though the listener may not feel the same way as the speaker, it still involves placing oneself in their position and understanding their point of view.

4. **Emotional Empathy:** - Sharing in the speaker's emotional experience takes emotional empathy a step further. It entails feeling some degree of the same emotions as the speaker and developing a deeper emotional connection with them.

5. **Avoiding Judgment:** - Communication that is empathetic is nonjudgmental. It entails putting aside preconceived notions and judgments in order to create a safe space where the speaker can express themselves without worrying about backlash.

1. **Transformative Effect on Communication Among People:**

a. **Establishing Trust:** - Empathy and attentive listening are key components in building trust in interpersonal relationships. People naturally develop trust when they feel acknowledged, heard, and understood; this builds the foundation for stronger connections.

b. **Handling Conflicts:** - In a confrontation, understanding opposing viewpoints requires both empathy and active listening. People are better able to negotiate conflicts and move toward resolution when they actively engage with opposing ideas and demonstrate empathy.

c. **Building Stronger Bonds with Others:** - Effective communication is a prerequisite for meaningful partnerships.

Empathy and active listening foster an atmosphere where people feel appreciated and understood, which strengthens emotional bonds.

d. **Improving Emotional Effectiveness:** Two essential elements of emotional intelligence are empathy and active listening. Gaining these abilities promotes better interpersonal connections, self-regulation, and emotional awareness.

e. **Promoting Diversity:** - Active listening and empathy promote inclusivity in varied and multicultural environments. People from varied origins can feel appreciated and included in an atmosphere when different viewpoints are acknowledged and understood.

f. **Enhancing Leadership Capabilities:** - Skillful leaders possess the ability to actively listen and communicate with empathy. By encouraging open communication, developing trust, and establishing a healthy company culture, these abilities improve leadership effectiveness.

g. **Promoting Openness:** - Empathy and attentive listening motivate people to communicate honestly. People are more inclined to talk honestly and openly when they believe that their ideas and feelings are valued and understood.

h. **Helping with Problem-Solving:** - Effective problem-solving in collaborative situations is facilitated by empathy and active listening. People can work together to explore solutions that meet the needs of all parties involved if they have a thorough awareness of the problems and viewpoints of each stakeholder.

i. **Promoting Personal Development:** - Listening intently and communicating with empathy can help people develop personally. People develop a mindset of perpetual learning and extend their comprehension of the world by remaining receptive to diverse viewpoints and experiences.

j. **Fostering Positive Environments:** - Positive and

collaborative environments are those that exhibit active listening and empathy. People experience encouragement and support, which boosts motivation and gives them a sense of community.

In summary, good communication elevates talks to transformative interactions through the use of active listening and empathy. The amalgamation of active listening and empathy, whether in interpersonal relationships, professional environments, or wider social contexts, generates a potent dynamic that cultivates trust, promotes comprehension, and advances personal development and well-being.

5.5 Developing Social Confidence and Charisma

Charm and social confidence are two traits that are crucial for both career and personal success. They enable people to make genuine relationships, move through social situations with ease, and make a good impression on others. The significance of charm and social confidence, techniques for fostering them, and the positive effects they can have on a range of facets of life are all covered in this section.

1. Realizing the Value of Charm and Social Confidence:

Charm and social confidence go hand in hand and are essential to interpersonal dynamics. Positivity about oneself and ease of interaction in social situations are key components of social confidence. Conversely, charisma is that alluring characteristic that captivates others and makes one seem interesting and captivating. When combined, these qualities support good relationship-building, leadership, and effective communication.

Important Elements of Social Confidence:

1. **Self-Image That Is Positive** - A positive self-image is the foundation of social confidence. It entails embracing a sound sense of self-worth, admitting flaws, and acknowledging one's virtues.

2. **Effective Communication Skills:** - The foundation of social confidence is clear and effective communication. This involves having the capacity for clear and concise thought, attentive listening, and genuine conversational engagement.

3. **Body Language:** - Social confidence is greatly influenced by nonverbal indicators like body language. A confident manner is enhanced by maintaining eye contact, adopting an open and relaxed stance, and using suitable movements.

4. **Resilience to Rejection:** - People who are socially secure can withstand criticism and rejection. They are aware that not every interaction will be met with acceptance, and they choose to learn from mistakes rather than allow failure to sap their self-esteem.

Important Elements of Charisma:

1. **Authenticity:** - Genuine and authentic interactions characterize charismatic people. Their honesty strikes a chord with others, fostering a feeling of connection because they are real to themselves.

2. **Confidence Without Arrogance:** - Confidence without arrogance is a hallmark of charisma. People that possess charisma radiate confidence while maintaining a kind and modest demeanor, allowing others to feel at ease in their company.

3. **Empathy:** - An essential element of charisma is empathy. People with charisma are sensitive to the feelings and wants

of others, which fosters a sense of comprehension and connection that extends beyond social encounters.

4. **Charismatic Presence:** - Having a magnetic presence that grabs attention is a common component of charisma. It can be communicated by combining warmth, assurance, and an engaging style of speaking.

1. **Techniques to Help You Gain Social Confidence:**

a. **Positive Affirmations and Self-Reflection:** - Reflect on your own strengths to recognize and value them. To support a good self-image, incorporate affirmations into your everyday practice.

b. **Gradual Exposure to Social Settings:** - Introduce yourself to social situations, even if they seem difficult, little by little. To gain confidence, start with smaller get-togethers and then advance to bigger ones.

c. **Create Powerful Communication Skills:** - Practice makes perfect in communication abilities. Pay attention to the capacity for precise thought and idea expression, attentive listening, and clear articulation.

d. **Accept Rejection as a Teaching Moment:** - Accept rejection as a normal aspect of social relationships. Rejection can help you improve your social abilities, so take advantage of it instead of letting it undermine your confidence.

e. **Seek Positive Feedback:** - Consult mentors or close friends for constructive criticism on your social interactions. Acknowledgment can bolster self-assurance and draw attention to areas in need of development.

f. **Enhance Body Language:** - Be mindful of your body language. To project confidence in social situations, practice keeping eye contact, using open gestures, and adopting a comfortable posture.

Growth Mindset Development: - Adopt a growth mindset that believes social skills are something that can be cultivated and enhanced over time. This kind of thinking encourages an openness to change and grow.

3. Methods for Creating Charm:

a. **Foster Authenticity:** - Adopt authenticity by staying loyal to who you are. Since authenticity is an essential component of charm, try not to take on a persona that seems distant from who you really are.

b. **Exercise Empathetic Listening:** - Gain the ability to listen with empathy. Be mindful of other people's viewpoints, acknowledge their emotions, and genuinely want to learn about their experiences.

c. **Focus on Approachability and Confidence:** - Strike a balance between approachability and confidence. Maintain a self-assured manner without becoming distant. Being approachable encourages people to get to know you personally.

d. **Create a Distinctive Presence:** - Create a distinctive presence that makes you stand out. This could be figuring out how to convey your uniqueness in social situations, adding comedy, or improving the way you communicate.

e. **Look for Leadership Opportunities:** - Take advantage of leadership opportunities in both professional and community contexts. Positions of leadership offer an opportunity to cultivate and exhibit charismatic traits.

f. **Strengthen Emotional Intelligence:** - Develop emotional intelligence by being aware of and in control of your own feelings as well as those of others. This improves your capacity to emotionally connect with others.

g. **Ongoing Education and Adjustment:** - View charisma as a lifelong process of education and adjustment. Remain receptive to criticism, be prepared to improve your social skills, and modify your strategy in response to various social settings.

4. Revolutionary Effect on Individual and Workplace Lives:

a. **Career Advancement:** - Charm and social confidence are factors in career progression. People who are adept at navigating social situations with confidence and cultivating positive relationships tend to stand out in the workplace, which presents chances for personal and professional growth.

b. **More robust networks of professionals:** - People with charisma typically develop more robust professional networks. Their interpersonal skills, capacity to inspire confidence, and ability to make a good impression make it easier for them to establish lasting professional partnerships.

c. **Enhanced Effectiveness of Leadership:** - Socially confident leaders

and charm are more useful for motivating and guiding groups. Their presence cultivates a favorable company culture, and their capacity to establish personal connections with people increases loyalty and trust.

a. **Healthful Interpersonal Connections:** - People with charm and social confidence frequently have deeper personal connections. Their capacity to be genuine in their interactions, listen with empathy, and project warmth helps to build deeper and more satisfying bonds.

b. **Enhanced Persuasion and Influence:** - People who are charismatic have an innate capacity for persuasion and influence. They are powerful communicators because of their assured and captivating demeanor and sharp communication abilities.

c. **Individual Development and Adaptability:** - Gaining charisma and social confidence requires personal development. It entails pushing past comfort zones, accepting obstacles, and developing perseverance in the face of failures.

d. **Beneficial Effect on Overall Health:** - People who are charming and self-assured in social situations frequently see improvements in their wellbeing. Overall life pleasure is influenced by one's capacity to establish deep connections and handle social situations with ease.

To sum up, cultivating charisma and social confidence is a life-changing experience that improves a variety of facets of both personal and professional life. Through fostering a positive self-perception, honing communication abilities, accepting genuineness, and forming compassionate relationships, people can improve their social presence and make a favorable, long-lasting impression on others they come into contact with. These characteristics are important assets in the quest of a fulfilling and well-rounded existence since they not only support professional achievement but also enhance and enrich interpersonal connections.

Chapter 6: Applying Emotional Intelligence in Work Environments

6.1 Leadership and Emotional Intelligence

The art of leadership is complex and goes beyond simple managerial duties. Proficient executives motivate and direct their groups, cultivating a favorable company environment and propelling group accomplishments. Emotional intelligence is a crucial characteristic that sets outstanding leaders apart. This section explores the mutually beneficial relationship between emotional intelligence and leadership, focusing on how emotional intelligence influences successful leadership and advances organizational greatness.

1. **Recognizing Emotional Intelligence's Function in Leadership:**

The ability to identify, comprehend, regulate, and make positive use of one's own and other people's emotions is known as emotional intelligence (EI). When it comes to decision-making, interpersonal interactions, and general team dynamics, emotional intelligence (EI) becomes a crucial factor in leadership. Emotionally intelligent leaders can create a good work atmosphere, lead their teams to top performance, and negotiate challenging situations with grace.

Emotional Intelligence in Leadership: Key Components:

1. **Self-Awareness:** - Leaders with high emotional intelligence are acutely conscious of their own feelings. They are able to recognize and comprehend their advantages and disadvantages as well as how their emotions affect their interactions and decision-making.

2. **Self-Regulation:** - Capable of controlling and regulating their emotions, self-regulation is exhibited by effective leaders. This entails controlling your emotions under duress, choosing wisely, and refraining from rash actions that can lower team morale.

3. **Motivation:** - Leaders that possess strong emotional intelligence and are motivated do it out of a love for what they do and a dedication to the success of their team. Their energy and ability to convey a compelling vision energizes and inspires others.

4. **Compassion:** - The foundation of emotional intelligence in leadership is empathy. Trust and collaboration are fostered

in a friendly and inclusive environment by leaders who are able to empathize with and understand their team members' emotions.

5. **Social Skills:** - Effective connection builders and maintainers are leaders with good social skills. They build a supportive team environment that promotes candid communication and collaboration, handle disagreements gently, and communicate clearly.

1. **How Effective Leadership Is Affected by Emotional Intelligence:**

a. **Better Decision-Making:** - Emotionally intelligent leaders make better choices. They can evaluate circumstances more thoroughly and make well-informed decisions if they are aware of their own emotions as well as those of others.

Enhancing Communication: **b.** One of the characteristics of emotionally savvy leaders is effective communication. They are able to communicate ideas clearly, actively listen to others, and modify their communication methods to appeal to a range of listeners.

a. **Fostering Cooperation and Trust:** - The foundation of all successful leadership is trust. Leaders with emotional intelligence establish trust by real concern for the welfare of their team members, sincerity, and consistency. This trust encourages teamwork and a feeling of unity.

b. **Handling Conflicts:** - Any workplace will inevitably experience conflict, but emotionally savvy leaders are adept at resolving it. They skillfully handle disagreements by focusing on comprehending the underlying causes and approaching problems with empathy, which promotes a positive work atmosphere.

c. **Employee Engagement and Motivation:** - Emotionally

intelligent leaders are able to relate to and comprehend the motives and difficulties of their team members. Employee motivation and engagement rise as a result of this relationship, and there is a common commitment to accomplishing company objectives.

d. **Flexibility in the Face of Change:** - Because of the dynamic nature of the business environment, executives must be adept at navigating change. Leaders that possess emotional intelligence are flexible and strong, steering their groups through changes while preserving spirits and optimism.

e. **Fostering a Positive Culture Within the Organization:** - A positive workplace culture is facilitated by emotional intelligence. Emotionally intelligent leaders promote inclusivity, diversity, and a work environment where people feel appreciated and encouraged, all of which contribute to a positive work environment.

f. **Handling Stress:** - Leadership positions frequently involve a lot of stress. Emotionally intelligent leaders are skilled at stress management, staying composed, and acting as a stabilizing force during trying times, all of which improve the well-being of the team as a whole.

3. How to Become an Emotionally Intelligent Leader:

a. **Self-Reflection:** - Regular self-reflection helps leaders improve their emotional intelligence. This entails analyzing one's emotional reactions, comprehending triggers, and pinpointing areas in need of development.

b. **Actively Seeking input:** - Getting input from mentors, peers, and subordinates can give one important insight into how others view their emotional intelligence. Growth and development opportunities are provided by constructive criticism.

c. **Training on Emotional Intelligence:** - Programs for developing leaders frequently incorporate instruction on emotional intelligence. These courses offer methods and resources to improve interpersonal, self-control, and self-awareness.

d. **Mindfulness activities:** - Deep breathing exercises and meditation are examples of mindfulness activities that can improve self-awareness and self-regulation. Including mindfulness in everyday activities promotes resilience and emotional well-being.

e. **Empathy Building Exercises:** - By participating in activities that promote perspective-taking, leaders may proactively hone and strengthen their empathy. This could entail paying attention to what team members have to say, making an effort to comprehend their perspectives, and accepting different points of view.

f. **Ongoing Education:** - The development of emotional intelligence is a lifelong talent. Throughout their careers, leaders who are dedicated to lifelong learning and personal growth are more likely to develop and fortify their emotional intelligence.

4. Emotional Intelligence and Leadership in the Future:

The importance of emotional intelligence in leadership is further highlighted by the fact that enterprises must traverse an ever more complicated and interconnected world. It is expected that leaders who can cultivate collaboration, adjust to change, and sensitively lead diverse, international teams will be given priority in the future of leadership. As technology advances,

Emotional intelligence is still a uniquely human quality that distinguishes leaders in their capacity to empathize, motivate, and guide.

Result:

To sum up, the foundation of effective and transformative leadership is the junction of emotional intelligence and leadership. Building strong, cohesive teams, fostering a healthy corporate culture, and navigating the obstacles of the modern workplace are all made easier for leaders who place a high priority on developing their emotional intelligence. The enduring significance of emotional intelligence guarantees that leaders who develop this skill set will be well-positioned for success in leading their organizations toward excellence even as leadership paradigms continue to change.

6.2 Creating Positive Workplace Culture through EI

A productive workplace culture is a valuable resource that supports worker happiness, engagement, and company success. The development and maintenance of a positive workplace culture are significantly influenced by emotional intelligence (EI). This section looks at how managers can use Emotional Intelligence (EI) to foster a culture of trust, cooperation, and a common goal.

Recognizing How Emotional Intelligence Affects Workplace Culture:

The ideas, beliefs, attitudes, and behaviors that characterize how people interact inside an organization are all included in the concept of workplace culture. The focus that emotional intelligence places on identifying and regulating emotions has a significant influence on how relationships function in the workplace as well as the culture at large.

Leaders with high emotional intelligence (EI) can shape the emotional atmosphere within the company, encouraging a work environment where staff members feel appreciated, encouraged, and inspired to give their all.

Emotional Intelligence as a Foundation for Workplace Culture:

1. **Leadership Empathy:** - Empathic leaders are able to comprehend and share the emotions of others. They have a high emotional intelligence (EI). This empathy is also shown to workers, resulting in a leadership approach that recognizes and responds to the range of feelings and experiences present in the workforce.

2. **Efficient Communication:** - Emotional intelligence (EI) improves communication abilities, allowing leaders to express ideas clearly and intelligently. Open communication inside the company is promoted, miscommunication is decreased,

and trust is built via transparent and compassionate communication.

3. **Dispute Settlement:** - Any workplace will inevitably experience conflict, but leaders with emotional intelligence are skilled at finding constructive solutions. They tackle disputes with empathy, making an effort to comprehend the underlying feelings and viewpoints of people involved, which promotes a constructive and cooperative conclusion.

4. **Stability and Flexibility:** Resilience and adaptability are important traits in a workplace that is changing quickly, and EI helps to develop both. Emotionally intelligent change managers instill confidence and foster an environment that rewards creativity and expansion.

5. **Team Collaboration:** - Leaders with high emotional intelligence are excellent at forming and leading teams. They foster teamwork, comprehend the intricacies of interpersonal interactions, and establish a welcoming atmosphere that values the skills and viewpoints of all people.

2. Techniques for Using EI to Develop a Positive Workplace Culture:

a. **Lead by Example:** - Leaders need to set an example for the attitudes and conduct they want to see in the workplace. Possessing a high emotional intelligence sets the bar for constructive relationships and motivates staff to reach it.

b. **Promote Open Communication:** - Establish an environment where staff members are at ease sharing their ideas and worries. Emotionally intelligent leaders actively listen to their team members, ask for comments, and make sure that everyone is heard.

c. **Offer Emotional Support:** - Acknowledge that workers bring their feelings to work. Emotionally intelligent leaders provide emotional support, empathetically addressing difficult situations and acknowledging accomplishments to foster a sense of belonging and recognition among coworkers.

d. **Give Employee Well-Being Priority:** - EI leaders give their employees' well-being top priority. This entails promoting work-life balance, taking into account the emotional impact of actions made at work, and putting work into projects that assist mental health and general wellness.

e. **Put Emotional Intelligence Training Programs into Practice:** - Include programs for developing emotional intelligence in professional development efforts. Through these programs, leaders and staff members can both improve their emotional intelligence (EI) skills, promoting a common understanding of EI inside the company.

f. **Promote Collaborative Decision-Making:** - Foster a collaborative decision-making environment. High EI leaders solicit feedback from their team members, include them in decision-making, and foster a sense of responsibility that enhances the work environment.

g. **Acknowledge and Reward Positive Behaviors:** - Give recognition to positive actions that fit the ideal company culture. Employees are encouraged to keep making valuable contributions to the company by receiving recognition, which strengthens the culture of gratitude.

h. **Encourage Inclusion and Diversity:** - Leaders in EI promote inclusivity and diversity. They respect and acknowledge the diversity of their staff, making sure that each person feels valued and able to provide their special insights to the company's success.

i. **Offer Growth Opportunities:** - Establish a culture that prioritizes lifelong learning and career advancement. Leaders with emotional intelligence (EI) assist staff members in growing professionally by offering chances for skill improvement and internal promotion.

j. **Establish Unambiguous Values and Expectations:** - Express the organization's values and expectations in a clear and concise manner. A common understanding of the ideal work environment is facilitated by leaders with emotional intelligence (EI) by ensuring that these ideals are consistent with a healthy company culture.

3. Transformative Effect on the Success of the Organization:

a. **Increasing Worker Engagement:** Employee engagement rises when a positive workplace culture is fostered via emotional intelligence. Workers who have an emotional connection to their jobs and company are more driven, effective, and dedicated to reaching common objectives.

b. **Higher Retention Rates:** - Talented individuals are more likely to be retained by companies with a positive workplace culture. High EI leaders foster a supportive and valued work environment, which lowers turnover and promotes long-term organizational success.

c. **Enhanced Originality and Imagination:** - Creativity and invention are encouraged in a culture that emphasizes emotional intelligence. Workers that work in an environment like this are encouraged to voice their opinions, take prudent risks, and add to the organization's innovative potential.

d. **Enhanced Organizational Reputation:** - Organizations with positive work environments and strong emotional intelligence (EI) leadership tend to have better reputations. In the cutthroat business world, this reputation draws in top personnel, cultivates a good rapport with partners and clients, and enhances overall success.

e. **Enhanced Performance and Productivity:**

● Workplace environments that prioritize emotional intelligence lead to increased output and effectiveness. Workers are more likely to succeed in their positions and add to the success of the company when they see emotionally intelligent leaders as motivating, understanding, and supportive.

a. **Greater Ability to Adjust to Change:** - Companies with

Positive and emotionally intelligent business cultures are more flexible. Both leaders and employees handle change with resilience, seizing new chances and facing obstacles together with a shared goal.

Result:

In conclusion, firms looking to achieve long-term success must strategically prioritize developing a pleasant workplace culture through emotional intelligence. Leaders that put employee well-being (EI) first foster a collaborative, communicative, and member-centered work environment. Increased creativity, better retention rates, better employee engagement, and a stronger reputation are all signs of the transformative power of EI on organizational success. The development of emotional intelligence in leadership turns into a competitive advantage and a major factor in driving organizational excellence as firms navigate a changing business environment.

6.3 Managing Teams and Collaboration Effectively

Collaboration and efficient team management are essential to the success of any firm. A successful leader is one who can unite disparate people, capitalize on their talents as a group, and steer them toward shared objectives. The main tactics for leading teams and encouraging cooperation are examined in this section, with a focus on the significance of leadership, communication, and trust-building in establishing high-performance team dynamics.

1. **Establishing a Trusting Foundation:**

The foundation of efficient team management is trust. Building trust between team members and between the team and its leader fosters a productive workplace where people feel safe, appreciated, and inspired. Leaders that exhibit integrity, are transparent, and consistent in building trust. Important Techniques for Establishing Trust:

1. **Transparent and Open Communication:** - Promote transparent and open communication among team members. Open communication among leaders fosters trust by informing team members about objectives, standards, and any changes that might affect their job.
2. **accountable:** - Encourage an environment in which team members accept accountability for their deeds and promises. When people keep their word, trust is built, resulting in a dependable and cohesive team.
3. **Equity and Fairness:** - Guarantee equity and fairness in the allocation of resources and decision-making. A sense of camaraderie is fostered and trust is strengthened when team members feel they are being treated properly.

4. **Recognition and Appreciation:** - Express gratitude to team members for their contributions. Acknowledging both individual and group efforts helps to maintain a positive team environment by fostering mutual respect and trust.

5. **Conflict Resolution:** - Handle disagreements quickly and amicably. By displaying a commitment to collaborative problem-solving, effective conflict resolution builds trust by demonstrating that challenges are treated seriously.

1. Efficient Methods of Communication:

Collaboration within the team requires good and transparent communication. To make sure that everyone in the team is on the same page, leaders need to set expectations, provide information, and encourage open communication. Furthermore, active listening fosters comprehension and strengthens bonds between people, making it an essential part of good communication.

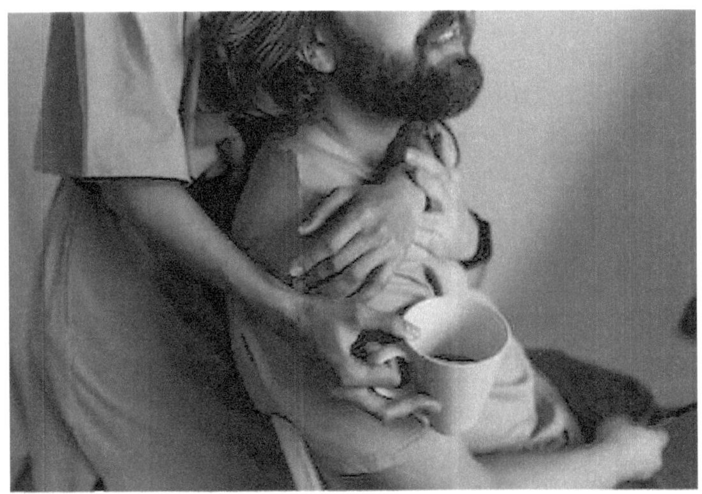

Principles of Successful Communication:

1. **Clearly Defined aims:** - Clearly state the expectations, aims, and objectives of the team. Communication becomes more in line with the team's direction and goals when everyone is aware of them, and activities are coordinated to achieve shared goals.
2. **Regular Team Meetings:** - Hold regular team meetings to go over updates, discuss issues, and review progress. Open communication is facilitated via meetings, which give team members a platform to exchange ideas, pose queries, and work well together.
3. **Use of Collaborative Tools:** - Make effective use of technologies and collaborative tools to facilitate communication. Project management, file sharing, and real-time messaging platforms facilitate collaboration and improve communication, particularly in distant or virtual team environments.
4. **Active Listening:** - Promote active listening among team members. Actively listening to team members shows respect, validates viewpoints, and fosters an environment of open communication.
5. **Feedback Mechanisms:** - Provide a system of feedback to promote ongoing development. Feedback that is constructive improves communication between team members, helps them identify areas for improvement, and aligns expectations.

1. **Promoting a Culture of Collaboration:**

Creating an atmosphere where team members feel empowered to exchange ideas, work together on projects, and solve problems as a group is essential to effective cooperation. Individual efforts alone are not enough. Shared ownership, inventiveness, and originality are all encouraged in a collaborative culture.

Principles for Promoting Collaboration:

1. **Team Building Activities:** - Plan team-building exercises to improve communication amongst team members. Whether they are conducted in person or virtually, team-building activities give members of the team a chance to interact personally and develop a spirit of cooperation.

2. **Encouraging Diverse Perspectives:** - Welcome different points of view and motivate team members to express them. A wide variety of perspectives fosters creativity, improves problem-solving, and makes for a more fulfilling collaborative experience.

3. **Cross-Functional Collaboration:** - Promote communication between various teams or departments to enable cross-functional cooperation. Cross-functional cooperation dismantles departmental silos, encourages knowledge exchange, and advances a more comprehensive comprehension of corporate objectives.

4. **Common Vision and Shared Goals:** - Ascertain that team members have a common vision and share goals. Collaboration gains significance when all members comprehend the overall goal and how their unique contributions support the team's accomplishment.

5. **Celebrating Achievements:** - Highlight group accomplishments and significant anniversaries. Acknowledging group accomplishments fosters a collaborative culture and supports the notion that cooperation produces fruitful results.

1. **Strengthening Team Leadership to Achieve Success:**

Leading a team to succeed requires strong leadership. Encouraging team members to realize their full potential, offering direction, and cultivating a healthy team culture are all components of an empowering leadership style. Teams with more empowerment are more flexible, resilient, and able to overcome obstacles.

Principles for Developing Leadership:

1. **Assigning Responsibilities:** - Assign tasks in accordance with the abilities and strengths of team members. Encouraging leaders who empower their team members to take on tasks and responsibilities instills a sense of accountability and ownership.

2. **Offering Growth Opportunities:** - Encourage team members' professional development. Leaders who offer chances for improvement, training, and promotion show that they care about the success of their team and the personal development of their members.

3. **Building a Safe Environment** - Create a psychologically secure atmosphere where team members are at ease sharing their thoughts and taking measured chances. A secure atmosphere fosters creativity and innovation, which promotes teamwork.

4. **Removing Obstacles:** - Find and eliminate roadblocks that prevent the team from moving forward. Teams may overcome barriers and accomplish their objectives when empowered leaders take an active approach to problem-solving, allocate resources, and foster a positive work environment.

5. **Leading by Example:** - Set an example for the team by acting in accordance with the values and conduct that are expected of them. Empowering leaders model the traits they want to see in their team members, setting the example for cooperation.

1. **Feedback and Ongoing Improvement:**

A dedication to ongoing development is necessary for effective team management. Leaders need to evaluate team dynamics on a regular basis, ask for input, and put initiatives into place to improve cooperation. Teams that adopt a continuous improvement culture are more likely to be resilient and adjust to changing difficulties.

Principles for Ongoing Enhancement:

1. **Regular Performance evaluations:** Evaluate team and individual performance through regular performance evaluations. Performance evaluations offer a platform to acknowledge accomplishments, tackle obstacles, and establish objectives for development.

2. **Feedback Loops:** - Create feedback loops to facilitate continuing dialogue. Frequent feedback—both official and informal—reinforces positive behavior, helps pinpoint areas that need work, and promotes an environment where learning never stops.

3. **Learning from Difficulties:** - See difficulties as teaching moments. In order to promote continuous improvement, leaders can help teams overcome challenges by guiding them through a process of reflection, learning, and adaptation.

4. **Adapting to Change:** - Encourage a flexible culture. Teams that are flexible in a business environment that is changing quickly

swiftly adapt to changing conditions and have a higher chance of success. When it comes to leading teams through uncertainty and change, leaders are essential.

1. **Team Training and Development:** - Make an investment in your team members' education and training. The team's capacity for adaptation and development is facilitated by skill development, industry trend monitoring, and the promotion of a culture of lifelong learning.

Leading teams and encouraging collaboration are dynamic, varied tasks that call for a blend of communication techniques, leadership abilities, and a dedication to ongoing development. Establishing a collaborative culture, empowering team members, adjusting to shifting conditions, and fostering trust are all essential components of effective team management. By putting these crucial tactics into practice, leaders can drive their teams toward high-performance dynamics, where people flourish, creativity blossoms, and organizational objectives are met through cooperation and teamwork.

6.4 Emotional Intelligence in Decision-Making at Work

A key component of successful leadership and organizational performance is effective decision-making. Decisions have an impact on everything from daily operations to long-term strategy in the dynamic and complicated workplace. Emotional intelligence (EI) becomes apparent as a critical component in the decision-making process, impacting how leaders manage their emotions, comprehend other people's viewpoints, and make decisions that balance human dynamics and organizational objectives.

1. Understanding How Emotions Affect Decision-Making:

Human experience is inherently emotional, and emotions have a significant influence on decision-making. Emotional intelligence in leaders is the awareness that feelings have the power to shape both their own and others' perceptions. It is essential to comprehend the emotional background of a decision in order to make decisions that respect people's wellbeing, preserve harmonious working relationships, and are consistent with the organization's ideals.

Principles of Emotional Intelligence in Making Decisions:

1. **Self-Awareness:** - Self-aware leaders are conscious of their own feelings and how they might affect the choices they make. They may approach decision-making with a thorough understanding of their emotional state and any biases thanks to their self-awareness.

2. **Empathy:** - Empathy is the capacity to comprehend and experience another person's emotions. Empathic leaders take into account the feelings and viewpoints of individuals impacted by a choice, encouraging a more inclusive and people-centered method of making decisions.

3. **Emotion Regulation:** - The ability to control one's emotions

is a component of emotional intelligence. Effectively controlling their emotions enables leaders to make more logical and impartial choices, even under duress.

4. **Social Skills:** - A facet of emotional intelligence, social skills comprise the aptitude for negotiating social circumstances and cultivating constructive connections. Socially adept leaders are able to convey decisions with empathy, which helps the team members comprehend and support the decision.

Including Emotional Intelligence in the Process of Making Decisions:

a. **Mindful Decision-Making:** - Making decisions with mindfulness entails being totally present and cognizant of one's thoughts and feelings. Before making decisions, leaders can benefit by pausing to think things through and make sure that feelings are taken into account.

b. **Emotional Impact Assessment:** - Take into account how decisions will affect the team's and each person's emotions. Recognizing that emotions may affect motivation, morale, and the culture of the workplace as a whole, leaders with strong emotional intelligence assess how decisions may be interpreted.

c. **Seeking Diverse Viewpoints:** When making judgments, emotionally intelligent leaders aggressively seek out different points of view. Leaders may make better decisions that take into account a wider range of perspectives by being aware of the feelings and opinions of their team members.

d. **Establishing a Positive atmosphere for Decision-Making:** Encourage open communication and psychological safety to create a positive atmosphere for decision-making. Leaders get important insights that help them make well-informed decisions when team members feel free to voice their ideas and concerns.

e. **Accepting Constructive Feedback:** - Accepting constructive feedback is a necessary component of emotional intelligence. Leaders that are receptive to criticism on their choices are better able to adjust and show that they are dedicated to lifelong learning and development.

3. Finding a Rationality-Emotion Balance:

Reason and emotion must be balanced in order to make effective decisions. Though emotions can offer insightful information, emotionally savvy leaders understand that decisions should also be supported by reasoned analysis. Achieving this equilibrium guarantees that choices are both strategic and sympathetic.

a. **Emotional Factors:** - Recognize and take into account the feelings that influence a choice. This entails being aware of the emotional impact on stakeholders, anticipating possible emotional responses, and empathetically handling problems.

b. **Rational Analysis:** - Evaluate the choice rationally, taking into account pertinent information, facts, and strategic ramifications. Leaders with emotional intelligence incorporate this analytical approach to guarantee that choices are based on a thorough comprehension of the circumstances.

c. **Collaborative Decision-Making:** Encourage important stakeholders to participate in collaborative decision-making processes. Diverse viewpoints are brought to the table through collaboration, which also helps divide the emotional burden of decisions and increase their collective ownership.

d. **Decision-Making Frameworks:** - Make use of frameworks for decision-making that take into account both rational and emotional aspects. Decision-making is given structure by models like the dual-process theory, which recognize the interaction between intuitive and analytical thinking.

4. Managing Feelings in Crucial Decisions:

Emotions are frequently running high when making important decisions, and the effects on people and the business can be profound. Emotionally intelligent leaders are adept at handling the emotional ramifications of important choices while maintaining the process's integrity, openness, and consideration.

a. **Emotional Readiness** - Leaders with emotional intelligence readied themselves to face the emotional obstacles associated with critical choices. This entails preparing for efficient communication, taking into account the emotional needs of individuals impacted, and foreseeing possible responses.

b. **Open Communication:** - Keep lines of communication open during the whole decision-making process. Even in difficult situations, leaders should establish trust by being transparent about information, explaining decisions and their reasoning, and responding to concerns in an open and honest manner.

c. **Offering Assistance:** - Acknowledge the effect on the team's emotions

members and offer assistance. In periods of major change or uncertainty, emotionally intelligent leaders provide resources, direction, and channels for voicing concerns. They are also sensitive to the welfare of their teams.

a. **Post-Decision contemplation:** - Practice post-decision contemplation following a critical decision. Leaders that possess emotional intelligence evaluate the emotional consequences, solicit input, and pinpoint opportunities for enhancement in upcoming decision-making procedures.

Result:

To sum up, emotional intelligence is a useful skill in the challenging world of professional decision-making. In addition to making strategic decisions, leaders who incorporate emotional intelligence into their decision-making processes foster settings where decisions are made with empathy and consideration for the effects on others. Emotionally intelligent leaders balance reason with emotion, understand the importance of emotions, manage high-stakes decisions skillfully, and promote the success of their organizations and the well-being of their staff. Emotional intelligence in decision-making is still crucial for navigating the complex dynamics of today's professional environment, even as workplaces continue to change.

6.5 Conflict Resolution Strategies in Professional Settings

Professional life will inevitably involve conflicts due to different viewpoints, conflicting interests, and different personalities at work. For both team leaders and members, effectively managing and resolving disagreements is an essential skill. The basic techniques for resolving conflicts in work environments are examined in this section, with a focus on the value of cooperation, communication, and a positive attitude in preserving a peaceful workplace.

1. **Recognizing the Types of Conflicts at Work:**

Recognizing the variety of workplace problems is crucial before diving into certain conflict resolution techniques. Differing communication styles, competing objectives, rivalry for resources, and even personal disagreements can all lead to conflicts. The first step in putting successful conflict resolution techniques into practice is to comprehend the underlying causes of conflicts.

Principles Concerning Workplace Conflicts:

1. **Differences in Communication:** - Misunderstandings or disruptions in communication are frequently the cause of conflicts. Team members may become tense due to miscommunication, misunderstandings, or differences in communication styles.

1. **Differing Viewpoints and Objectives:** Team members may disagree in their priorities, viewpoints, or objectives. Tension and discord result when these distinctions are not acknowledged or appreciated, giving birth to conflicts.

2. **Competition for Resources:** - When there is rivalry for scarce resources, such as time, money, recognition, or other necessary components for a successful team, conflicts may occur at work.

3. **Interpersonal Dynamics:** - Conflicts can arise from differences in personalities and interpersonal dynamics. Tension within a team can be caused by clashing personalities, unsolved personal difficulties, or personal biases.

1. **Active Management of Conflicts:**

Although confrontations are unavoidable, proactive steps can be done to lessen or avoid their effects. It is possible for team leaders and members to cultivate a productive workplace that emphasizes cooperation, respect, and open communication.

Principles for Preventing Conflict:

1. **Open and Clear Communication:** - Promote open and transparent communication among team members. Creating open lines of communication makes sure that everyone is in agreement and helps avoid misunderstandings.

2. **Establishing Explicit Expectations:** - Clearly state expectations as well as roles and responsibilities. Ambiguity lessens the chance of disagreements amongst team members when they are clear about their responsibilities and roles.

3. **Cultivating a Positive Team Culture:** - Encourage a collaborative, diverse, and inclusive team culture. Healthy relationships are built on a foundation of mutual respect and understanding, which is fostered by a positive culture.

4. **Conflict Resolution Training:** - Give team leaders and members conflict resolution training. Giving people the tools they need to handle conflict constructively helps keep small arguments from turning into big problems.

1. **Useful Techniques for Resolving Conflicts:**

When disagreements do occur, it's critical to resolve them quickly and amicably. Professional settings can benefit from the following dispute resolution techniques:

a. **Paying Attention:** - One of the fundamental techniques in conflict resolution is active listening. Make sure that everyone feels understood and heard. This entails summarizing, paraphrasing, and seeking clarification in order to fully comprehend each person's viewpoint.

b. **Collaborative Problem-Solving:** Promote a cooperative method of addressing problems. Rather than concentrating on placing blame, identify solutions that will work for everyone concerned. Working together to solve problems promotes a feeling of shared accountability and ownership.

c. **Mediation:** - When disputes get out of hand, think about having a third party who is impartial mediate. Mediators can assist in guiding conversations, facilitating communication, and assisting in the search for amicable solutions.

d. **Creating Ground Rules:** - Create guidelines for resolving disputes within the team. These guidelines can include acting professionally, refraining from insulting others, and resolving to solve problems rather than assign blame.

e. **Stressing the Value of Emotional Intelligence:** - To resolve conflicts, emotional intelligence is essential. To foster empathy and understanding during the conflict resolution process, teach team members how to identify and control their emotions.

f. **Addressing Core Issues:** - Move past minor arguments and deal with the fundamental problems that are causing the conflict. Investigating underlying worries, unfulfilled wants, or unsolved historical issues that are impacting the current conflict may be part of this.

g. **Promote Sincere Apologies and Forgiveness:** - Promote genuine apologies in circumstances when they are appropriate. Similarly, encouraging forgiveness in the workplace enables team members to put aside disagreements and concentrate on working together.

h. **Escalation Procedures:** - Define precise procedures for handling disputes that can't be settled inside the team. Conflicts are handled at the proper organizational level when parties know when and how to escalate them.

4. Reflection and Learning After Conflict:

It is beneficial to reflect and learn after a conflict has been resolved. This procedure entails assessing the conflict resolution tactics employed, pinpointing areas in need of development, and putting policies in place to stop recurring disputes.

Important Aspects of Reflection After Conflict:

1. **

Debriefing: - Hold a debriefing meeting following a dispute resolution. This enables team members to voice any unresolved issues, discuss their viewpoints on the settlement process, and offer suggestions for enhancements.

1. **Identifying Root Causes:** - Contemplate the main reasons behind the disagreement. Comprehending the fundamental problems aids in averting relapses and facilitates focused measures to tackle systemic problems.
2. **Learning and Adaptation:** - Promote an environment where learning and adaptation are ongoing processes. Utilize the knowledge acquired from resolving conflicts to improve team procedures, communication tactics, and conflict avoidance techniques.

Professional situations necessitate a diverse approach to conflict resolution that includes preemptive steps, practical tactics, and a dedication to continuous learning. Teams may create a supportive and cooperative work atmosphere where individuals can flourish and differences are respected by resolving conflicts in a constructive manner. By placing a strong emphasis on collaborative problem-solving, mediation, active listening, and post-conflict reflection, disputes are not only settled but also help the team and the organization as a whole develop and become more resilient.

Chapter 7: Emotional Intelligence in Relationships

7.1 Improving Intimate Relationships through EI

The complex and multidimensional nature of intimate relationships necessitates a careful balancing act between emotional intelligence, clear communication, and mutual support. Improving the durability and quality of close relationships is largely dependent on emotional intelligence (EI). This section looks at how enhancing intimate relationships through the use of emotional intelligence (EI) principles can lead to stronger connections, empathy, and a harmonious partnership.

1. Identifying One's Own and Others' Emotions:

Self-awareness is the foundation of emotional intelligence, which also includes the ability to identify and comprehend the emotions of others. This self-awareness establishes the groundwork for candid and open communication in close relationships.

Important Elements of Emotion Recognition:

1. **Self-Awareness:** - People with high emotional intelligence are aware of their own feelings. They are able to recognize and communicate their emotions, which is essential for communicating needs, wants, and worries in a partnership.

2. **Empathy:** - Empathy is a fundamental component of emotional intelligence that entails sharing and comprehending the emotions of others. Empathetic partners are able to establish a closer emotional bond and deeper connection with their significant ones in intimate partnerships.

3. Honest and Transparent Communication:

The foundation of strong intimate relationships is effective communication. Communication is improved by emotional intelligence because it encourages vulnerability, openness, and attentive listening.

Principles for Honest and Open Communication:

1. **Emotional Expression:** - High EI partners find it easy to communicate their feelings. This fosters an atmosphere in which both parties may express their ideas, emotions, and worries without worrying about being judged.

2. **Active Listening:** - An essential part of emotional intelligence is active listening. Actively listening partners show respect, acknowledge one another's emotions, and foster an environment conducive to candid and insightful communication.

3. **Avoiding Assumptions:** - People with emotional intelligence are better able to avoid assuming the best about their partner's intentions or sentiments. Rather, they ask questions in order to get clarification and have discussions that advance comprehension.

4. **Using "I" Statements:** - Framing communication with "I" statements rather than critical "you" remarks promotes accountability and avoids placing blame. For instance, stating "I feel" as opposed to "You always" directs attention away from placing blame and into personal feelings.

1. **Controlling and Handling Feelings:**

Not only can emotional intelligence be used to identify emotions, but it can also be used to efficiently manage and regulate them. Being able to handle emotional highs and lows is important for maintaining stability in close relationships.

Important Elements of Emotional Management:

● **Emotional Regulation:** - Partners with high emotional intelligence are able to control their feelings and refrain from acting impulsively. This control over emotions keeps arguments from getting worse and enables more deliberate reactions.

2. **Stress Management:** - External stressors frequently arise in intimate relationships. Stress is something that people with emotional intelligence (EI) can handle well, keeping it from ruining a relationship. Resilient relationships depend on resilient coping strategies like support and communication.

1. **Fostering Understanding and Empathy:**

A fundamental component of emotional intelligence, empathy can be a potent instrument for fostering understanding and connection in close relationships.

Important Techniques for Developing Empathy:

1. **Putting Oneself in the Other's Shoes:** - Partners with high emotional intelligence (EI) are able to put themselves in their partners' shoes and view circumstances from their point of view. Partners' emotional link is strengthened and compassion is fostered by this empathic understanding.

2. **Validating Emotions:** - In close partnerships, emotional validation is essential. When partners affirm one other's feelings, they recognize the importance of those feelings and help to create an atmosphere of emotional safety and understanding.

1. **Emotional Intelligence in Conflict Resolution:**

Any relationship will inevitably encounter conflicts, but how those conflicts are resolved can have a big influence on the partnership's overall health. A person with emotional intelligence is equipped with constructive dispute resolution techniques.

Important Techniques for Resolving Conflicts:

1. **Remaining Calm:** - People with high EI are able to maintain composure and calmness in the face of conflict. This emotional restraint keeps disagreements from turning into heated disputes and promotes more reasoned problem-solving.

2. **Finding Solutions:** - Emotional intelligence encourages a dispute resolution strategy that is solution-focused. Partners with high emotional intelligence collaborate to identify practical solutions that deal with core problems rather than lingering on past transgressions or placing blame.

1. **Fostering Emotional Closeness:**

Being emotionally close to someone transcends being physically close. It entails disclosing one's weaknesses, worries, and dreams. To foster this kind of closeness, emotional intelligence is essential.

Important Elements of Developing Emotional Closeness:

1. **Vulnerability Sharing:** - High EI partners are comfortable disclosing their weaknesses. Because both parties can trust each other with their most private thoughts, this openness fosters a safe environment in which emotional intimacy can grow.

2. **Celebrating Successes and Challenges:** - Emotional intelligence makes it possible for partners to sincerely acknowledge and encourage one another through difficult times. The emotional connection between people is strengthened by this shared experience.

1. Introspection and Ongoing Development:

People who score well on emotional intelligence reflect on themselves and understand the value of ongoing personal and interpersonal development.

Important Elements of Self-Reflection:

1. **Personal Growth:** - Emotional intelligence promotes personal growth by getting people to think critically about their own actions and feelings. In the framework of the relationship, this self-awareness helps one become a more developed and healthy version of themselves.

2. **Adaptability:** - High EI partners are flexible and eager to develop their relationship with one another. The connection is stronger when both parties can adjust to shifting conditions and overcome obstacles.

To sum up, emotional intelligence is a great tool for enhancing close relationships. People can establish a foundation of trust, understanding, and emotional intimacy in their relationships by identifying and controlling their emotions, encouraging open communication, developing empathy, and constructively resolving problems. As long as people are dedicated to personal and relational development and engage in ongoing self-reflection, Emotional Intelligence will be a driving force behind the development of vibrant, strong, and close-knit intimate partnerships.

7.2 Parenting with Emotional Intelligence

It takes a profound awareness of oneself, one's children, and the dynamics of family relationships to be a parent, but it is also a wonderful and challenging journey. The holistic method of parenting with emotional intelligence (EI) places a strong emphasis on communication skills, empathy, and managing one's own and the children's emotions. In order to promote good family dynamics, robust parent-child relationships, and healthy emotional development, this section delves into the ideas and practices of parenting with emotional intelligence.

Recognizing the Fundamentals of Emotional Intelligence in Parenting:

Recognizing, comprehending, and controlling emotions in both parents and children are fundamental components of emotionally intelligent parenting. Among the fundamental ideas are:

Main Tenets of Emotionally Intelligent Parenting:

1. **Self-Awareness:** - Parents with high emotional intelligence are conscious of their own feelings and responses. They are able to set an example of appropriate emotional management for their children because they are self-aware.

2. **Empathy:** - The foundation of EI in parenting is empathy. It entails identifying and comprehending the sentiments of a child, confirming those feelings, and reacting to them in a compassionate manner.

3. **Effective Communication:** - Parents with emotional intelligence are able to communicate with their kids in an effective way. This calls for attentive listening, honest emotional expression, and the capacity to constructively communicate boundaries and expectations.

4. **Emotion Regulation:** - Parents with emotional intelligence are able to control their own emotions, which helps them avoid impulsive behavior and give their kids a secure emotional environment.

2. Forming Emotional Connections:

A good parent-child connection is built on the emotional ties that bind parents and children together. Emotionally intelligent parenting centers on fostering these connections via satisfying emotional encounters.

Key Techniques for Creating Emotional Connections:

1. **Quality Time:** - Developing emotional ties with children requires spending quality time with them. This entails participating in activities together, giving your all, and making

happy memories that you can both enjoy.

2. **Expressing Affection:** - A crucial element of emotional bonding is expressing love and affection. Acts of compassion, physical gestures, and verbal affirmations all help a youngster feel safe and included.

3. **Celebrating Achievements:** - No matter how tiny, praising and acknowledging a child's accomplishments helps to build a strong emotional bond. The child gains confidence and feels validated by this acknowledgment.

4. **Supporting Through Challenges:** - Parents with emotional intelligence offer assistance when things go tough. Building trust in the parent-child relationship and assisting youngsters in navigating challenging emotions are two benefits of providing comfort, direction, and assurance.

3. Accepting Guidance from Emotions:

A parenting strategy called "emotional coaching" entails guiding kids through their feelings and assisting them in comprehending and controlling them.

Important Elements of Emotional Mentoring:

1. **Identifying and Validating Feelings:** - Acknowledging and affirming a child's feelings is the first step in providing emotional support. This entails accepting the child's feelings without passing judgment on them.

2. **Open Communication:** - It's important to have honest conversations regarding feelings. By fostering a comfortable environment for conversation, emotionally intelligent parents support their kids in expressing their emotions.

3. **Educating Emotional Control:** - Part of emotional coaching involves educating kids on how to control their emotions. This entails offering coping techniques, problem-solving abilities, and approaches to stress or frustration management.

4. **Collaborative Problem-Solving Together:** - An essential component of emotional coaching is collaborative problem-solving. Children are empowered when they work together to discover answers and are reminded that emotions can be managed in a healthy way.

1. **Establishing Well-Being Boundaries:**

Setting and upholding appropriate limits is a key component of emotionally intelligent parenting. Children feel more secure when there are defined boundaries, and they also learn self-control and responsibility.

Principles of Healthy Boundaries:

1. **Consistency:** - It's important to be consistent while establishing and upholding boundaries. Consistency is exhibited by emotionally competent parents, giving their kids a clear idea of what is expected of them and what happens when they don't meet them.

2. **Explaining Reasons:** - Emotionally savvy parents give explanations for boundaries rather than just imposing arbitrary rules. This promotes understanding, and when kids understand why the rules are in place, they're more likely to follow them.

3. **Promoting Self-Sufficiency:** - A healthy set of limits also permits a certain amount of age-appropriate freedom. Parents that are emotionally savvy find a balance between offering direction and letting their kids explore and gain knowledge from their experiences.

4. **Respecting Individuality:** - Part of establishing appropriate limits for a child is acknowledging and appreciating their uniqueness. Parents that possess emotional intelligence recognize that every child is different and may have varying

needs and preferences.

1. Emotional Intelligence Role Modeling:

The parents are the children's main role models. Children's emotional navigation skills are shaped by adults who model emotional intelligence through their own behavior.

Important Role Modeling EI Aspects:

1. **Managing Stress:** - Effective stress management is modeled by parents with emotional intelligence. Youngsters pick up coping mechanisms from watching their parents, which serves as a model for appropriate stress management.
2. **Problem-Solving Skills:** - Children that exhibit these abilities learn how to tackle difficulties methodically. Children who have emotionally intelligent parents participate in the process, encouraging resilience and a sense of competence.
3. **Expressing Emotions Appropriately:** - Parents should set an example for acceptable emotional expression. Parents who possess emotional intelligence model for their children that it's acceptable to experience a wide range of emotions and that politely expressing them is a virtue.
4. **Apologizing for Mistakes:** - Parents with emotional intelligence own up to their errors and extend their regrets. Children learn from this that everyone makes mistakes and that accepting responsibility for one's actions is a virtue.

1. Promoting Self-Sufficiency and Adaptability:

The goal of EI parenting is to help kids become resilient and independent. This entails supporting them while motivating them to acquire the abilities and perspective required to overcome obstacles in life.

Principal Techniques for Promoting Self-Sufficiency and Adaptability:

1. **Encouraging Decision-Making:** - Independence is fostered when children are encouraged to make decisions that are acceptable for their age. Parents that possess emotional intelligence offer direction while letting their kids make their own decisions.
2. **Teaching Skills for Solving Problems:** - Teaching problem-solving

-solving abilities provide kids the confidence to take on obstacles. Children who have emotionally intelligent parents are assisted in creating efficient problem-solving techniques.

1. **Positive Reinforcement:** - A child's confidence is increased when they receive positive reinforcement for their efforts and accomplishments. Parents that possess emotional intelligence place more emphasis on the process than the final product.
2. **Coping with Setbacks:** - One of the key components of resilience is the ability to deal with setbacks. Children who have emotionally savvy parents learn to see setbacks as chances for improvement and education.

Result:

A dynamic and compassionate parenting style that takes into account the emotional health of both parents and kids is known as emotional intelligence parenting. Parents may build a nurturing and supportive environment for their children to thrive in by modeling positive behaviors, establishing appropriate boundaries, encouraging emotional attachments, and adopting the ideas of emotional intelligence. When emotional intelligence is used to parenting, it helps create emotionally strong, self-assured, and compassionate people who are capable of navigating life's challenges.

7.3 Navigating Social Circles and Enhancing Friendships

Developing friendships and navigating social circles are complex life skills that call for a combination of emotional intelligence, empathy, and social skills. Creating and preserving deep friendships is a major factor in a person's overall happiness, personal development, and well-being. This section delves into tactics and ideas for thriving in social circles, creating real connections, and improving the caliber of friendships.

1. Being Aware of Social Dynamics

Social circles are intricate webs of connections, each with its own peculiar dynamics. People must understand the nuances of social interactions, such as group dynamics, communication styles, and the elements that lead to satisfying social experiences, in order to successfully navigate these circles.

Important Considerations for Comprehending Social Dynamics:

1. **Observation and Adaptability:** - Sharp observation and adaptability are the first steps towards successfully navigating social circles. People who are aware of the dynamics of a group might modify their conduct and communication style to better suit the social setting.
2. **Cultural Sensitivity:** - In varied social groups, cultural sensitivity is essential. Comprehending and honoring cultural subtleties fosters a peaceful interpersonal atmosphere and helps prevent miscommunications or inadvertent transgressions.
3. **Identifying Social Cues:** - It's critical to be able to identify and decipher social cues. This entails being aware of subtle cues, group norms, and nonverbal communication in order to help people navigate social circumstances with grace.
4. **Developing Social Self-Belief:** - Overcoming social anxiety and cultivating a positive self-image are necessary for gaining social confidence. Being confident makes it easier for people to interact with others, which helps them succeed in traversing different social circles.

1. **Promoting Sincere Bonds:**

The foundation of meaningful friendships is shared experiences, trust, and authenticity. Building mutual respect, transparency, and understanding at the core of social circles is essential to fostering true connections.

Principles for Developing Sincere Relationships:

1. **Authenticity:** - Meaningful relationships are built on the foundation of being sincere and authentic. Being genuine builds relationships inside the social circle by fostering trust and inspiring others to be authentic as well.
2. **Attentive Hearing:** - The ability to actively listen is essential

for developing real connections. It entails giving talks your whole attention, exhibiting empathy, and genuinely caring about the opinions and feelings of people.

3. **Common Values and Interests:** - Establishing shared values and interests improves relationships. Social circles can be a strong place to establish and maintain friendships because of shared experiences and interests.

4. **Openness and Vulnerability:** - Building deeper friendships requires being vulnerable and open. Building trust by the sharing of one's innermost feelings, ideas, and experiences inspires others to do the same, which results in deeper connections.

1. Handling Social Difficulties:

Social circles are bound to provide difficulties, including disagreements, miscommunications, or shifts in the dynamics of the group. It takes emotional intelligence, skillful communication, and conflict resolution to navigate these obstacles effectively.

Principles for Handling Social Difficulties:

1. **Dispute Settlement:** - In social relationships, conflict is inevitable. Conflicts are approached constructively by emotionally intelligent people, who look for solutions through compromise, open communication, and empathy.

2. **Effective Communication:** - Navigating social issues requires clear and effective communication. In social settings, disputes can be resolved by listening intently to others' viewpoints and expressing oneself assertively but respectfully.

3. **Adaptability to Change:** - A number of variables can cause social circles to change over time. People that are flexible manage changes in their social circles more easily, whether it is in group dynamics or personal relationships.

4. **Developing Empathy:** - Empathy is essential for comprehending the feelings and viewpoints of others. Building empathy enables people to handle social situations delicately and promotes harmonious connections within the group.

1. Fortifying Virtual Friendships:

Social circles in the digital age encompass online friendships in addition to those that are physically close. Effective communication in a digital setting is one of the special factors needed to navigate and improve these virtual connections.

Principles for Developing Virtual Friendships:

1. **Digital Etiquette for Communication:** - In order to maintain online friendships, one must comprehend digital communication etiquette. Positive relationships in virtual social circles are facilitated by succinct and clear messaging, considerate behavior when interacting online, and tone awareness.

2. **Regular Engagement:** - Maintaining an online friendship requires regular engagement. Frequent communication via text, phone conversations, or video chats keeps people feeling connected and fortifies their relationship even when they are physically separated.

3. **Halving Relationships Between Online and Offline:** - Although friendships made online are valuable, it's important to balance them with in-person interactions. Arranging face-to-face gatherings whenever feasible fosters stronger bonds and gives the friendship a depth of common experiences.

4. **Digital Empathy:** - In online encounters, digital empathy is taking others' sentiments into consideration. Understanding the constraints of digital communication and using virtual

channels to communicate empathy are important aspects of maintaining the health of online friendships.

1. Fostering Friendships for Life:

Friendships that last a lifetime are valuable assets that need to be intentionally maintained. Putting money into these relationships means keeping in touch on a regular basis, acknowledging achievements, and adjusting to life's shifting circumstances.

Important Techniques for Developing Lifelong Friendships:

1. **Consistent Check-Ins:** - It's crucial to stay in touch with lifelong friends on a regular basis. To stay in touch, this could be writing a kind note, picking up the phone, or organizing sporadic get-togethers.
2. **Celebrating Milestones:** - Long-lasting connections are strengthened when milestones, both personal and professional, are acknowledged and celebrated. Honoring birthdays, anniversaries, or noteworthy accomplishments shows how much value is placed on the friendship.
3. **Adjusting to Shifts in Life:** - Adapting to life's changes is essential for maintaining long-lasting connections. This could be acknowledging changing priorities, encouraging friends through difficulties, and acknowledging each other's life transitions.
4. **Solicitation and Support for One Another:** - Establishing a foundation of mutual support and encouragement is essential for enduring friendships. Friendships are forged through shared experiences and trust, which can only be achieved by supporting one another through good and bad times.

Emotional intelligence, social skills, and a sincere desire to create lasting relationships are all necessary for navigating social circles and maintaining friendships. Through comprehending social dynamics, creating sincere connections, empathetically navigating social problems, and fortifying virtual friendships,

and fostering enduring relationships, people can build a diverse web of social ties that enhance their general sense of well-being and contentment with life. The ideas of efficient navigation and relationship enhancement are still very important in helping people feel connected and at home in the ever-evolving web of human relationships, even when social circles change.

7.4 Handling Difficult Conversations with Emotional Intelligence

In life, difficult talks will inevitably arise in both personal and professional contexts. These discussions could cover sensitive subjects, resolve disputes, or offer constructive criticism. To navigate these difficult conversations effectively, one must possess a high degree of emotional intelligence (EI). In order to promote positive outcomes, we emphasize empathy, active listening, and constructive communication in our discussion of techniques for managing challenging discussions with EI.

1.   Acknowledging the Feelings at Play:

It's important to identify and accept the emotions involved before engaging in a challenging conversation, for both the other person and oneself. Conversational tone and outcome are greatly influenced by emotions.

Important Elements of Emotion Recognition:

1. **Awareness of Oneself:** - High EI people are self-aware and able to recognize their own feelings. Consider your own emotions and any potential biases that might affect the topic before striking up a difficult talk.
2. **Empathy:** - Empathy entails sharing and comprehending the emotions of others. To approach the conversation with compassion and consideration, you must first recognize the feelings of the person you are conversing with.
3. **Cultural Sensitivity:** - Variations in culture can affect how emotions are perceived and communicated. Being sensitive to cultural differences enables people to handle challenging conversations by being aware of the range of emotional

responses.

1. **Getting Ready for the Talk:**

One of the most important aspects of managing tough talks is preparedness. This entails defining goals, foreseeing difficulties, and planning how to keep a polite and productive conversation going.

Most Important Preparation Techniques:

1. **Define Objectives:** - Clearly state what you want to get out of the discussion. When discussing a difficult problem, offering criticism, or resolving a conflict, the dialogue is guided by a clear grasp of the intended results.
2. **Anticipate Reactions:** - Prepare for potential responses from the opposite side. It is possible to better prepare and adapt during the conversation by taking into account various points of view and possible emotional reactions.
3. **Select the Appropriate Setting:** - The setting in which the discussion occurs is very important. Select an environment where there are no interruptions, open conversation is encouraged, and both people feel free to express themselves.
4. **Script Key Points:** - Although the discussion should flow naturally, using a script or outline for key points guarantees that crucial information is understood and that the discussion stays on topic.

1. **Listening intently and giving sympathetic answers:**

The cornerstones of managing challenging conversations with EI are attentive listening and sympathetic answers. Engaging completely with the speaker and reacting in a way that shows empathy and comprehension are key components of active listening.

Principles of Empathic Reactions and Active Listening:

1. **Pay Close Attention:** - Steer clear of outside distractions and focus entirely on the speaker. This shows consideration and fosters an atmosphere that encourages candid dialogue.

2. **Paraphrase and Summarize:** - Summarizing and paraphrasing what the other person has said demonstrates your interest in learning about their viewpoint and your active listening skills.

3. **Validate Emotions:** - Recognize and accept the feelings that the other person has stated. Emotional validation fosters trust and makes room for more candid and open communication.

4. **Use "I" Statements:** - When discussing your personal ideas and emotions, utilize "I" statements to explain your viewpoint without coming across as critical. For instance, use "I feel" rather than "You always."

1. **Keeping Your Emotions Under Control:**

One of the most important skills for managing challenging talks with EI is emotional management. It entails controlling one's own emotions and reacting to difficult or emotionally intense conversations in a cool, collected manner.

Important Elements of Emotional Control:

1. **Pause and Breathe:** – If the discussion gets heated, stop for a while and relax. This little break helps people control their emotions and avoid impulsive behavior.

2. **Remain Calm and Composed:** - Throughout the conversation, keep your composure. People with emotional intelligence can respond carefully and handle tension, which makes for a more positive conversation.

3. **Treating Emotional Escalation:** - If feelings become more intense, deal with the emotional side of things first. Recognize the heightened feelings, show empathy, and steer the

discussion back toward a more positive direction.

4. **Know When to Take a Break:** - Determine when a break is required, if necessary. Retaking the topic at a later time after taking a step back can help both sides recover their composure.

1. A Solution-Oriented Method:

Emotional intelligence is characterized by a solution-focused approach to challenging conversations. Instead of focusing only on the problems, together seek out positive solutions.

Important Elements of a Solution-Focused Method:

1. **Collaborative Problem-addressing:** - Promote the practice of addressing problems together. Emotionally intelligent people work together to discover answers, stressing the value of coming to an agreement.
2. **Focus on the Future:** - Recognize the problems of the past but direct attention to what is ahead. Talking about the future and making constructive adjustments makes the discussion more solution-focused and forward-thinking.
3. **Mutual Commitment:** - Verify that both sides are dedicated to reaching a favorable conclusion. Mutual commitment creates a sense of shared accountability for the discussion's results.
4. **

Follow-Up Actions: - Summarize the discussion by stating duties and next steps. Clearly defined future steps show a commitment to resolving the issues addressed and help to provide a sense of closure.

1. Contemplating the Discussion:

After the challenging discussion is over, give yourself some time to consider and assess yourself. By thinking back on the exchange, one can develop personally, hone communication abilities, and get better at handling difficult conversations in the future.

Important Points to Consider While Analyzing the Conversation:

1. **Self-Reflection:** - Consider the contributions you have made to the discussion. Think about the techniques used to control emotions, the success of the communication tactics, and the areas that still need work.

2. **Feedback Requesting:** - Ask the other person for their thoughts. Gaining insight from their point of view during the conversation can help shape future exchanges.

3. **Identifying Learning Points:** - List the lessons that you took away from the discussion. What was effective and what could be made better? For upcoming challenging conversations, apply these lessons to improve your emotional intelligence and communication abilities.

4. **Continuous Improvement:** - Adopt an attitude of ongoing development. Every hard talk is a chance for learning, and the lessons gained help one's ability to handle tough conversations with emotional intelligence in the future.

Result:

Emotionally intelligent handling of challenging interactions is a talent that may be honed over time. People can successfully manage difficult conversations by identifying their emotions, being well-prepared, actively listening with empathy, controlling their emotions, taking a solution-focused approach, and reflecting after the discussion. Incorporating emotional intelligence into challenging talks improves interpersonal connections and fosters a more positive and peaceful social and work environment. People who practice these techniques get good at transforming difficult talks into chances for learning, understanding, and constructive change.

7.5 Building Trust and Emotional Bonds in Relationships

Emotional ties and trust are the cornerstones of healthy, long-lasting relationships. The capacity to build and maintain trust is a key factor in the strength and durability of relationships, both in personal and professional settings. We examine the essential components of creating emotional connections and trust in this investigation, highlighting the value of open communication, empathy, vulnerability, and shared experiences in creating deep connections.

1. Communication as the Foundation:

The foundation of developing trust and strong emotional ties in relationships is open and honest communication. In addition to expressing oneself, effective communication also entails actively listening to others, promoting understanding, and establishing a secure environment for sincere conversation.

Important Communication Elements:

1. **Attentive Hearing:** - Effective communication is based on active listening. It entails paying close attention to what they have to say, making an effort to grasp their viewpoint, and intelligently answering. A sincere interest in the thoughts and feelings of the other person is communicated through active listening.

2. **Transparency and Clarity:** - Trust is fostered by communication that is transparent and clear. Minimizing misunderstandings and fostering an atmosphere of openness in the partnership are achieved via the clear expression of thoughts, feelings, and expectations.

3. **Empathetic Communication:** – An essential component of communication is empathy. Gaining insight into and acceptance of the feelings of the other person strengthens the emotional ties in a relationship and promotes a deeper level of connection.

4. **Constructive Feedback:** - Offering respectfully worded constructive criticism shows a dedication to both parties' development. By highlighting the common objective of mutual personal and interpersonal growth, constructive criticism enhances trust when it is given with empathy and an eye toward betterment.

1. Fostering Compassion and Perception:

One essential element of emotional ties in relationships is empathy. It entails having the capacity to empathize with and comprehend the emotions of others, establishing a strong bond and mutual support.

Important Techniques for Fostering Empathy:

1. **Perspective-Taking:** - Take an active role in considering other people's perspectives in order to comprehend their feelings and experiences. Considering things from their

perspective improves empathy and fortifies emotional ties.

2. **Emotional Validation:** - Expressing empathy and understanding by validating the other person's emotions. Whether or not your thoughts align with theirs, acknowledging them helps them feel heard and welcomed.

3. **Open-Mindedness:** - Have an open mind when engaging in discussions. A relationship can be more inclusive and sympathetic when both parties are receptive to diverse viewpoints and experiences.

Take part in and share in emotional experiences that are **shared**. Experiencing happy or difficult times together strengthens the emotional ties and forges enduring relationships.

1. The Power of Vulnerability:

Being vulnerable is a great way to foster emotional connections and trust. An atmosphere of closeness and honesty is fostered by being open to sharing one's vulnerabilities, experiences, and true self.

The Principal Facets of Vulnerability:

1. **Open Sharing:** - Be honest about your feelings, ideas, and personal experiences. In order to build trust, vulnerability entails taking down barriers and letting the other person see the real you.

2. **Admitting Errors:** - Own up to your mistakes and accept responsibility. Acknowledging flaws and growing from mistakes shows humility and fosters trust by indicating a dedication to one's own development.

3. **Expressing demands:** - Clearly state your expectations and demands. Being vulnerable in a relationship promotes mutual respect and a deeper knowledge of one another's needs and desires.

4. **Mutual Vulnerability:** - Promote mutual vulnerability by fostering an atmosphere in which both parties feel comfortable expressing who they really are. A sense of oneness is fostered and emotional relationships are strengthened through shared vulnerability.

1. Exchanged Memories and Experiences:

Creating and sharing experiences with one another is a big element of developing emotional connections. Big or small, shared memories build a collective history that fortifies the bond between the two people.

Important Features of Shared Experiences:

1. **Quality Time:** - Make time for each other. Taking part in happy and fulfilling activities makes memories with others and improves emotional relationships.
2. **Celebrating Milestones:** - Commemorate successes and landmarks with one another. A sense of collaboration and common objectives is fostered by celebrating and acknowledging shared accomplishments.
3. **Navigating Challenges Together:** - Overcoming obstacles as a group strengthens the bond between partners. A relationship is formed via sharing experiences and providing support to one another throughout trying times.
4. **Building Traditions:** - Create customs or rites exclusive to the partnership. Whether it's a yearly trip, a regular date night, or just a basic routine, establishing traditions helps people feel connected and consistent.

1. Stability and Trustworthiness:

Building trust requires a number of crucial components, including consistency and dependability. Establishing trustworthiness through words and deeds makes the other person feel safe and dependable in the connection.

Important Aspects of Dependability and Consistency:

1. **Keeping Promises and Commitments:** - Honor your word. Maintaining punctuality while making promises, no matter how minor, builds trust and strengthens confidence.

2. **Reliability in Emergencies:** - Show dependability when things go tough. Providing assistance and being there during trying times strengthens the emotional ties in the partnership.

3. **Consistent Communication:** - Ensure that you communicate consistently. A feeling of closeness and emotional intimacy can be fostered by routinely checking in and showing care, even in tiny ways.

4. **Reliability in Confidentiality** - Maintain trust and confidentiality. Building a foundation of trust and emotional comfort in a partnership begins with respecting the privacy and confidences exchanged.

Result:

Relationships require a dynamic and deliberate process to develop trust and emotional ties. People build and strengthen their relationships through emphasizing open communication, developing empathy, accepting vulnerability, sharing experiences, and acting consistently and dependably. These fundamental components foster interpersonal relationships and provide a safe haven where people can grow emotionally and improve one another's quality of life. Building emotional ties and trust during a relationship's development is a constant source of fulfillment, understanding, and support for both parties.

Chapter 8: Self-Discovery and Growth

8.1 Embracing Change and Adaptability

One of the most important components of resilience and personal development is learning to embrace change. People who have an open and flexible mentality not only flourish in the face of obstacles but also skillfully traverse transitions in a world that is always changing. In this investigation, we explore the importance of accepting change, the advantages of flexibility, and methods for cultivating an optimistic outlook on life's unavoidable changes.

1. **Recognizing the Character of Change:**

Life is full of inherent and ongoing change. Change can come in many forms, whether it be in the personal or professional realm. These forms include transitions, obstacles, chances, and viewpoint changes. Developing a mindset that accepts life's inherent dynamic nature begins with acknowledging that change is inevitable.

Critical Elements of Change Understanding:

1. **Inevitability of Change:** - The human experience is characterized by natural and inevitable change. When people accept that change is a necessary part of life, they are better equipped to handle it.
2. **Varieties of Shift:** - Change can take many different forms, ranging from internal changes in attitudes and beliefs to external events. Accepting change entails being receptive to the opportunities it presents as well as recognizing its many forms.
3. **Opportunity for Growth:** - Change offers chances for both professional and personal growth, even in its most difficult manifestations. Change becomes a road for self-improvement rather than a possible cause of concern when it is seen as a catalyst for growth.

1. Advantages of Flexibility:

There are several advantages to being adaptable—that is, having the capacity to thrive in the face of change. People who practice adaptation improve their ability to solve problems, their resilience, and their general well-being in addition to being more adept at navigating changes.

Primary Advantages of Flexibility:

1. **Resilience in Adversity:** - People who are adaptive show resilience in the face of difficulty. They overcome difficulties by coming up with innovative and practical solutions, growing stronger and more resourceful in the process.
2. **Improved Problem-Solving Skills:** - Effective problem-solving and adaptability go hand in hand. People who are adaptable approach problems with a solution-focused mentality, making use of their versatility to identify creative and useful solutions.

3. **Better Open-Mindedness:** - Being open-minded is facilitated by accepting change. People that are more adaptable are more open to fresh concepts, different viewpoints, and unconventional methods, which leads to a more vibrant and dynamic mental environment.

4. **Enhanced Emotional Welfare:** - The capacity for adaptation enhances emotional health. Accepting change promotes acceptance and serenity in the midst of ambiguity in life by lowering resistance and anxiety.

1. Methods for Getting Over Change:

Creating a mindset that welcomes change requires deliberate tactics that foster resilience and adaptability. These techniques enable people to move through changes with assurance and hope.

Principles for Accepting Change:

1. **Cultivate a Growth attitude:** - Adopt a growth attitude that views obstacles as chances for improvement and education. Growth mindsets encourage adaptability and a positive outlook on change.

2. **Practice Mindfulness:** - Being completely present and engaged in the present moment is a mindfulness practice that improves adaptation. People who are aware of the current moment can react to changes more calmly and clearly.

3. **Create a Supportive Network:** - Surround yourself with a network of friends, family, and coworkers who are there to support you. During times of change, a robust support network offers both practical and emotional help.

4. **Set Achievable Goals:** - Establish attainable goals. Adapting to change becomes less daunting and more reachable when bigger goals are divided into smaller, more achievable tasks.

1. Handling Changes in Workplace Environments:

Change is a constant in the professional world, whether it takes the shape of business trends, organizational reorganizations, or advances in technology. Having a proactive and adaptable mindset is necessary for accepting change in the job.

Important Techniques for Handling Career Transitions:

1. **Continuous Learning:** - Give skill development and ongoing education top priority. Professionals that are adaptable regularly look for opportunities to learn new skills and remain current in a constantly changing workplace.
2. **Adaptability in tasks:** - Show adaptability in your tasks and duties. Professionals that are flexible are willing to take on new tasks and modify their responsibilities to suit the demands of the company.
3. **Effective Communication:** - Continue to communicate with coworkers and supervisors in an honest and open manner. Taking the initiative to disseminate information and keeping up with organizational changes fosters adaptation in the workplace.
4. **Agile Decision-Making:** - Acquire the ability to make agile decisions. Professionals that are flexible make well-informed judgments quickly, taking into account how their workplace is changing.

1. In terms of Personal Development, Resilience:

Navigating life transitions, whether they be related to relationships, relocation, or lifestyle adjustments, is a crucial part of accepting change on a personal level. For personal development to succeed in the face of these changes, resilience is essential.

Main Techniques for Building Resilience in Personal Development:

1. **Introspection and Assessment:** - Practice introspection and assessment on a regular basis. Knowing one's own values, priorities, and objectives helps one become more adaptable by giving one a solid basis on which to make decisions when things change.

2. **Embrace Novel Experiences:** - Look for challenges and new experiences. On a personal level, accepting change means actively looking for chances for development, inquiry, and self-discovery.

3. **Mindful Coping Strategies:** - Create coping mechanisms that are mindful. Deep breathing exercises and other mindfulness techniques help people manage their emotions and deal with the stress that comes with transition.

4. **Build Resilient Relationships:** - Foster relationships that are resilient by emphasizing understanding and support for one another. A solid support network improves emotional health and offers a base for managing life transitions.

A transformative mentality that enables people to flourish in a world that is always changing is one that embraces change and adaptability. Through comprehension of the essence of change, acknowledging the advantages of flexibility, using techniques to manage shifts, and cultivating resilience in both personal and professional domains, people can confront life's ups and downs with assurance and hope. Accepting change is more than just responding to outside changes; it also entails deliberately developing a mindset that sees change as a necessary component of the path to innovation, personal development, and lifetime learning.

8.2 Personal Development Practices

A lifetime path of self-discovery, growth, and skill and quality upgrading is known as personal development. People who intentionally engage in behaviors that support personal growth are better equipped to realize their full potential, accomplish their objectives, and have more rewarding lives. We examine important personal development techniques in this investigation, such as developing self-awareness, accepting lifelong learning, and forming routines that support overall wellbeing.

1. Developing Introspection:

Self-awareness is the cornerstone of human growth. Gaining insight into one's values, beliefs, abilities, and shortcomings is essential for purposeful personal development. It takes introspection, contemplation, and a willingness to delve into one's inner landscape to develop self-awareness.

Important Elements in Developing Self-Awareness:

1. **Reflection Practices:** - Make reflection a frequent part of your life. Journaling, meditation, or other contemplative practices that promote reflection and self-discovery may be part of this.
2. **Feedback Seeking:** - Make a conscious effort to get input from others. Views from outside sources might provide insightful observations about facets of oneself that are not always obvious.
3. **Mindfulness and Present-Moment Awareness:** - Make use of present-moment awareness and mindfulness. There is a greater comprehension of one's thoughts, feelings, and behaviors when one is totally present in the moment.

4. **Self-Assessment and Strengths-Based Tools:** - Learn about strengths-based tools and personality evaluations. These resources offer organized frameworks for comprehending unique characteristics and attributes.

1. **Planning and Goal-Setting:**

Establishing attainable goals is essential to personal growth. Objectives offer guidance, inspiration, and a path forward. Establishing SMART (specific, measurable, attainable, relevant, and time-bound) goals is a necessary step in effective goal setting.

Important Aspects of Planning and Goal Setting:

1. **Clarity of Objectives:** - Clearly state your goals, both personal and professional. Setting goals that are clear aids in maintaining concentration and coordinating activities with the overall vision of the person.
2. **Breakdown into Actionable Steps:** - Divide more ambitious objectives into more manageable steps. This method facilitates a sense of accomplishment along the road and makes growth more achievable.
3. **Regular Progress Evaluation:** - Review progress on a regular basis and make necessary goal adjustments. Since personal development is a dynamic process, goals must be regularly evaluated to stay relevant.
4. **Long-Term Vision:** - Match immediate objectives with long-term objectives. Establishing a link between short-term goals and a longer-term vision gives direction and consistency.

1. **Ongoing Education and Talent Acquisition:**

A mindset of constant learning must be adopted in order to advance personally. Intellectual growth and adaptability are enhanced by actively searching out opportunities to gain new experiences, knowledge, and abilities.

Critical Elements of Ongoing Education and Talent Development:

1. **Formal and Informal Education:** - Take part in both kinds of education. While informal learning through reading, online courses, and practical experiences broadens viewpoints, formal education offers organized information.

2. **Skill Assessments:** - Determine and evaluate the abilities required for both career and personal development. Create a plan for using focused learning activities to acquire or improve these abilities.

3. **Mentorship and Networking:** - Look for chances to network and receive mentorship. Personal and professional development are facilitated by networking and learning from the experiences of others.

4. **Embrace Challenges as Learning Opportunities:** - View obstacles as chances to gain knowledge. Resilience and a growth attitude are fostered when failures are seen as teaching opportunities.

4. Habits for Health and Well-Being:

A person's mental and physical health are essential to their personal growth. Maintaining health through regular exercise, stress reduction, and mindful practices promotes long-term energy, clarity, and happiness.

Important Elements of Practices for Health and Well-Being:

1. **Regular Exercise Schedule:** - Include regular exercise in your everyday schedule. Engaging in physical activity not only enhances physical health but also has a favorable effect on mental health.

2. **Mental Eating Practices:** - Developmental eating practices. Making conscious dietary decisions and eating with purpose promote general health and energy.
3. **Adequate Sleep:** - Make getting enough good sleep a priority. Sleep is necessary for resiliency generally, emotional stability, and cognitive performance.
4. **Stress Reduction Techniques:** - Put these strategies into practice. This could be practicing deep breathing techniques, meditation, or other relaxation-oriented activities.
5. **Managing Your Time to Be More Productive:**

Productivity enhancement and efficient time management are essential components of personal development. Making the most of their time is possible when techniques for work prioritization, boundary setting, and efficiency optimization are put into practice.

Important Aspects of Productivity and Time Management:

1. **Prioritization of Tasks:** - Arrange tasks according to their urgency and importance. This makes it easier for people to concentrate on goal-aligned, high-impact activities.
2. **Efficient Planning and Scheduling:** - Put efficient planning and scheduling procedures into action. Productivity is increased when everyday chores are broken down and time is set aside for each activity.
3. **Setting Boundaries:** - To safeguard private and concentrated work time, set up distinct boundaries. Limiting distractions and unnecessary activities helps to guarantee times set out for focused work.
4. **Periodic Review and Adjustments:** - Evaluate productivity tactics on a regular basis and make necessary modifications.

Continuous practice improvement is necessary for personal development in order to maximize effectiveness.

6. Fostering Emotional Quotient:

A crucial element of personal growth is emotional intelligence (EI). Getting better at identifying, comprehending, and controlling one's own feelings as well as navigating interpersonal dynamics successfully is a key component of improved relationships and general wellbeing.

Important Elements of Emotional Intelligence Development:

1. **Emotional Self-Reflection:** - Reflect on your own feelings to gain an understanding of them. Emotional intelligence begins with awareness of one's own emotional terrain.
2. **empathic knowledge:** - Develop a knowledge of other people's feelings that is empathic. Interpersonal ties are strengthened as one learns to identify and address the emotions of others.
3. **Conflict Resolution Skills** - Learn how to resolve conflicts. Healthy relationships are facilitated by the skillful handling of problems through empathy and open communication.
4. **Continuous Improvement in Communication:** - Focus on making communication better all the time. Interactions both personally and professionally are improved by clear and compassionate communication.

Practices for personal development take a diverse approach to addressing several aspects of a person's life. These activities form an integrated framework for human progress, ranging from developing self-awareness and defining meaningful goals to prioritizing well-being, acquiring new skills continuously, managing time effectively, and fostering emotional intelligence. Participating in these deliberate pursuits enhances not only personal achievement but also leads to a more meaningful and satisfying existence. When people make a commitment to their continuous growth, they set out on a path of self-exploration and metamorphosis, realizing their full potential and appreciating the richness of a meaningful life.

8.3 Cultivating a Growth Mindset

A growth mindset is a potent psychological paradigm that modifies how people view obstacles, failures, and personal growth. The term "growth mindset," which was first used by psychologist Carol S. Dweck, contrasts with "fixed mindset," highlighting the idea that aptitude and intelligence may be enhanced via commitment, education, and perseverance. In this investigation, we examine the value of developing a growth mindset, how it affects both personal and professional goals, and methods for encouraging this paradigm-shifting viewpoint.

1. Being Aware of the Growth Mindset

A growth mindset is based on the idea that skills and abilities can be developed throughout time rather than being permanent attributes. People that have a growth attitude rise to challenges, see setbacks as teaching moments, and persevere in the face of difficulties. This kind of thinking affects not just how people tackle things but also how they react to criticism and how committed they are to doing better.

Critical Elements of the Growth Mindset:

1. **Embracing Challenges:** - People who have a growth mentality view obstacles as chances to improve. Instead than running away from challenges, they confront them head-on with interest and resolve.

2. **Learning from Setbacks:** – People see setbacks as a normal aspect of learning. Failure does not deter those with a growth mindset; rather, it presents an opportunity for growth, adaptation, and learning.

3. **Effort as the Path to Mastery:** – It is acknowledged that effort leads to mastery. People with a growth mindset know that consistent effort and dedication result in continual improvement rather than depending only on natural aptitudes.

4. **Embracing Feedback:** - Positive criticism is valued and regarded as a vital instrument for growth. People that have a growth mentality use criticism to improve their performance and hone their abilities.

1. **Effect on Individual Growth:**

Developing a growth mindset has significant effects on one's ability to progress personally. It fosters an atmosphere in which people are more likely to take on obstacles, endure hardships, and actively look for chances to learn and grow.

Important Elements of the Effect on Personal Growth:

1. **Openness to Learning:** - People who have a growth mindset are naturally receptive to new information. They actively seek out novel encounters, pick up fresh abilities, and consistently increase their body of knowledge.

2. **Enhanced Sturdiness:** - One characteristic of a growth mindset is resilience. People with this perspective don't let failures stop them; instead, they use the lessons learned from

them to overcome obstacles in their path.

3. **Adaptability in the Face of Change:** - People who possess a growth mindset are better able to deal with change. They are more likely to welcome change, see it as a chance for improvement, and modify their plans as necessary.

4. **Incentives for Ongoing Improvement:** - An innate drive for constant progress is fostered by a growth mentality. A person's desire to improve their skills and knowledge becomes their motivation for both personal and professional endeavors.

1. Effect on Career Objectives:

A growth mentality affects how people approach their jobs, communicate with coworkers, and overcome obstacles in the workplace. Innovation, teamwork, and resilience are frequently higher in organizations that promote a growth mindset culture. Important Elements of the Effect on Professional Pursuits:

1. **Creativity and Innovation:** - A growth mindset promotes creativity and innovation. People are more inclined to experiment, take calculated chances, and support an innovative work environment.

2. **Collaborative Teams:** - Individuals with a growth mentality are more likely to form collaborative teams. A culture where team members encourage one another's development is fostered by the emphasis on learning and improvement.

3. **Effective Leadership:** - A growth attitude is frequently in line with effective leadership. Leaders who have faith in their own and their team's capacity for personal growth and development foster cultures that encourage creativity and productivity.

4. **Resilience during Difficulties:** - Professional obstacles are confronted with fortitude. People who have a growth

mentality are more likely to see obstacles as temporary, endure through difficult circumstances, and approach problem-solving from a solution-oriented perspective.

4. Methods for Promoting a Growth Mentality:

A growth mindset must be continuously developed by deliberate effort and the formation of specific habits. A growth mentality can be fostered in many facets of both personal and professional life.

Principles for Developing a Growth Mindset:

1. **Embrace Challenges Actively:** - Seek out challenges and perceive them as chances for growth and development. Accepting obstacles increases one's comfort zone and develops a resilient mindset.
2. **Learn from Setbacks:** - Consider mistakes and setbacks to draw insightful conclusions. Consider the lessons that can be learnt and the ways that future efforts might be modified rather than focusing only on the bad parts.
3. **Cultivate Curiosity:** - Develop an inquisitive mindset. Ask inquiries, keep an open mind, and be willing to venture into new areas when you encounter new things.
4. **Assessment as

A Route to Mastery:** - Reorient the emphasis from natural aptitude to the work necessary for mastery. Realize that the secrets to constant progress are perseverance, practice, and commitment.

1. **Promote a Positive Relationship with Feedback:** - Accept criticism as a tool for development. Consider comments as a chance to improve performance and hone abilities rather than as a source of criticism.
2. **Set Realistic Goals:** - Make sure your goals are both hard and realistic. Stretching oneself to reach new heights motivates

one and paves the way for continued improvement.

3. **Create a Growth-Minded Environment Around Yourself** - Assemble a group of people who share your growth mindset. A community's collective thinking shapes individual viewpoints and promotes a constant improvement culture.

A growth mindset can be developed through a transforming process that benefits both professional and personal development. People can change their perspective and realize their potential for ongoing development by actively accepting difficulties, growing from failures, cultivating curiosity, acknowledging effort as a means of mastery, and promoting a positive relationship with feedback. A growth mentality has an effect on groups, companies, and eventually the larger culture in addition to individual pursuits. Communities and individuals that make a commitment to developing a growth mindset foster circumstances that support creativity, adaptability, and a shared dedication to lifelong learning and development.

8.4 Overcoming Self-Limiting Beliefs

Self-limiting beliefs are firmly held ideas about oneself that impede one's ability to reach one's full potential and impede personal development. These ideas, which are frequently based on unpleasant memories from the past or low self-esteem, erect mental obstacles that affect a person's ability to pursue a job, maintain healthy relationships, and generally feel good about themselves. It takes a transforming process that includes developing a mindset that promotes empowerment and possibilities, confronting negative thought patterns, and self-awareness to overcome self-limiting beliefs. We examine the nature of self-limiting ideas, their effects on people, and methods for overcoming these mental barriers in this investigation.

1. Comprehending Beliefs That Limit Oneself:

Subconscious convictions that influence a person's ideas, behaviors, and decisions are known as self-limiting beliefs. These ideas are frequently the result of negative reinforcement from repeated encounters, social conditioning, or early life events. Beliefs about one's value, aptitude, and chances for success are typical examples. They serve as mental barriers that prevent people from seizing chances, taking calculated chances, or realizing their full potential.

Critical Elements of Self-Limiting Belief Understanding:

1. **Rooted in Fear and Negative Conditioning:** - Fear and negative conditioning are common causes of self-limiting beliefs. Beliefs that impede human development can arise as a result of past experiences or cultural messaging.

2. **Influence on Thoughts and Behavior:** - These beliefs have an impact on how people think and act. People who hold negative self-limiting ideas may shy away from difficulties,

oppose change, or doubt their own talents as a result of these limitations.

3. **Impact on Goal Setting and Achievement:** - Self-limiting beliefs have a big influence on both of these processes. People can establish objectives that coincide with their limiting beliefs, which can result in a vicious cycle of unrealized dreams and unrealized potential.

4. **Self-Fulfilling Prophecy:** - Beliefs that restrict oneself have the potential to become self-fulfilling. When people act as though they are unworthy or unable, it might unintentionally reinforce these attitudes.

1. **Recognizing and Displacing Limiting Beliefs:**

Recognizing and identifying self-limiting beliefs is the first step towards conquering them. Honesty, introspection, and a readiness to question deeply ingrained mental patterns are necessary for this process. Once recognized, these viewpoints can be methodically refuted and replaced with ones that are more empowering. Important Pointers for Recognizing and Displacing Self-Limiting Beliefs:

1. **Awareness and Self-Reflection:** - Examine yourself to find self-limiting ideas. To start a shift, one must become conscious of the ideas and stories that reinforce restrictions.

2. **Interrogating Adverse Thought Patterns:** - Make an effort to challenge Adverse Thought Patterns. Asking whether self-limiting ideas are supported by data, prior experiences, or erroneous assumptions might help you refute their validity.

3. **Seeking Different Viewpoints:** - Look for different viewpoints. Examine how others might interpret comparable circumstances and confront the skewed perspectives that fuel self-limiting ideas.

4. **Cognitive Restructuring:** - Apply strategies related to

cognitive restructuring. Positive phrases and affirmations that challenge self-limiting ideas should be used to replace negative mental patterns.

1. Fostering an Attitude of Growth:

Overcoming self-limiting ideas requires developing a growth mentality. The idea that skills and intelligence may be developed via commitment and perseverance is emphasized by a growth mindset. Adopting this way of thinking encourages self-determination and an openness to growth.

Important Elements of Developing a Growth Mindset:

1. **Embracing obstacles as Opportunities:** - See obstacles as chances for personal development. People with a growth mindset are encouraged to view challenges as opportunities to learn new abilities and skills rather than as insurmountable roadblocks.

2. **Learning from Failures:** - Acquire knowledge from mistakes and setbacks. Those with a growth mindset use failure as a springboard for advancement rather than internalizing it as proof of their limitations.

3. **work as a Path to Mastery:** - Acknowledge that mastery requires a significant amount of work. A growth mindset replaces the idea that talent comes naturally to the concept that consistent hard work and commitment result in ongoing improvement.

Promoting Positive Self-Talk: - Encourage constructive self-talk. Affirmations and remarks that bolster confidence in one's capacity to overcome obstacles and accomplish goals should take the place of self-limiting language.

1. **Requesting Assistance and Input:**

It might be difficult to overcome self-limiting attitudes, but asking for help from others can be enlightening and motivating. Friends, mentors, or licensed counselors can provide direction, helpful criticism, and other viewpoints.

Important Elements of Requesting Assistance and Input:

1. **Creating a Supportive Network:** - Assemble a group of people who are committed to your personal development. The effect of self-limiting beliefs can be mitigated by surrounding oneself with good influences.
2. **Expert Advice:** - Take into account obtaining expert advice. Professionals such as therapists, coaches, or mentors can offer specific assistance in dispelling ingrained beliefs and provide methods for personal growth.
3. **Constructive Feedback:** - Welcome and consider criticism. Feedback from others can challenge self-limiting ideas and provide insightful information about one's areas of strength and progress.
4. **Accountability relationships:** Establish relationships for accountability. In order to overcome self-limiting beliefs, it can be helpful to have a companion with whom to discuss objectives and advancement.

1. **Creating and Reaching Gradual Objectives:**

Setting and completing small goals is a common step in overcoming self-limiting attitudes. Begin with modest, doable goals that correspond with your own desires. A person's narrative can be progressively changed and their confidence in their capacity to overcome obstacles can grow when they achieve these little achievements.

Prospects of Establishing and Reaching Gradual Objectives:

1. **Identifying Small Steps:** - Divide more ambitious objectives into more manageable steps. Finding doable projects increases a person's sense of success and strengthens their confidence in their capacity to advance.

2. **Celebrating Achievements:** - Honor accomplishments, regardless of size. Rewriting the story of self-limitation and providing positive reinforcement are two benefits of acknowledging success, even in small victories.

3. **Adjusting Goals as Needed:** - Be adaptable while making goal adjustments. The ability to adjust is essential for conquering self-limiting ideas, and people should have the confidence to modify their objectives in light of changing viewpoints.

4. **Maintaining a Growth attitude in Goal Pursuit:** - All through the goal pursuit, keep a growth attitude in place. Reiterating the positive momentum obtained from goal achievements, approach obstacles with a belief in one's capacity for growth and improvement.

Becoming self-aware, making conscious efforts, and dedicating oneself to personal development are necessary for the transforming process of conquering self-limiting beliefs. People can overcome mental limitations and realize their full potential by realizing the nature of these beliefs, confronting negative thought patterns, developing a growth mindset, getting help, and setting small, achievable goals. People continuously confront self-limiting ideas as part of an ongoing process that paves the road for a more powerful and satisfying existence. Breaking free from self-imposed constraints is a powerful driver for positive transformation and building resilience in the face of adversity in the pursuit of personal development.

8.5 Pursuing Continuous Self-Improvement

Constant self-improvement is a dynamic, lifelong process that is defined by deliberate attempts to raise one's level of knowledge, abilities, and general wellbeing. This commitment, which is based on the idea that personal growth is a continuous process, entails a number of intentional behaviors and practices meant to help people reach their full potential, build resilience, and adjust to the constantly shifting demands of life. We explore the importance of seeking continuing self-improvement, the fundamental ideas that direct this process, and useful techniques for navigating the road of constant personal development in this investigation.

2. The Importance of Ongoing Self-Improvement

A philosophy known as "continuous self-improvement" acknowledges the erratic character of human development. It recognizes that lifelong learning and development are essential components that go beyond certain objectives or turning points.

Adopting this way of thinking gives people the ability to overcome obstacles, take advantage of chances, and live more purposeful and happy lives.

Principal Elements of the Importance of Ongoing Self-Improvement:

1. **Stability in a Changing Environment:** - Adaptability is an important talent in a world that is changing quickly. People who are constantly improving themselves are able to adapt to change, remain flexible, and face uncertainty head-on.

2. **Reach Your Maximum Potential:** - The goal of constant self-improvement is realizing one's greatest potential. To attain the best possible results for both personal and professional goals, it entails recognizing strengths, resolving deficiencies, and consciously developing abilities.

3. **Improved Well-Being and Satisfaction:** - People who consistently work on improving themselves frequently express greater levels of happiness and contentment with their lives. A more meaningful and happier existence is gained from the sense of purpose and progress that come from continuous improvement.

4. **Cultivation of a Growth Mindset:** - Constant self-improvement is consistent with the growth mindset's tenets. Important elements of this transformational attitude include accepting obstacles, seeing failures as teaching moments, and being focused on personal growth.

2. Fundamental Ideas Underpinning Ongoing Self-Improvement:

A compass for purposeful growth, foundational principles steer the road of constant self-improvement. These guidelines offer a framework that helps people move purposefully and clearly through their developmental journeys.

Principles Fundamental to Ongoing Self-Improvement:

1. **Awareness and Self-Reflection:** - Constant self-improvement is based on self-reflection. It entails reflection, a sincere evaluation of one's own advantages and disadvantages, and knowledge of one's own ideals and goals.

2. **Planning and Goal-Setting:** - It's critical to establish attainable goals. Objectives offer guidance, inspiration, and a plan of action on the journey toward ongoing improvement. Planning effectively entails dividing more ambitious goals into smaller, more doable tasks.

3. **Commitment to Learning:** - The key to ongoing self-improvement is a dedication to lifelong learning. Inquisitiveness, learning new things, and curiosity are the seeds of intellectual development and flexibility.

4. **Welcoming Adaptability and Change:** - Accepting change is a fundamental idea. Adaptability to changing situations, viewpoints, and obstacles is essential for continuous personal growth.

5. **Resilience in the Face of Setbacks:** - This is an important quality. People who are always working on improving themselves are aware that obstacles are a necessary part of the process. They overcome obstacles, grow from experiences, and recover from setbacks.

1. **Doable Techniques for Ongoing Self-Improvement:**

Maintaining a state of constant progress in oneself calls for doable tactics that people can use to their everyday lives. These techniques cover a wide range of personal development topics, including emotional fortitude, physical health, and intellectual advancement.

Workable Techniques for Ongoing Self-Improvement:

1. **Regular Self-Assessment:** - Evaluate yourself on a regular basis to see how you're doing and to pinpoint areas that need work. This entails being open and honest about successes, failures, and how one's actions match their principles.

2. **Learning Plans and Skill Development:** - Create learning plans that include sections dedicated to improving skills. Determine which knowledge or skill gaps exist and develop a plan for filling them through workshops, courses, or practical experience.

3. **Reading and Ongoing Education:** - Develop a practice of ongoing education via reading. Investigate a variety of subjects, even ones that are not directly related to your area of expertise, in order to increase your knowledge and pique your curiosity.

4. **Mental and Physical Well-Being:** - Give your mental and physical health first priority. Maintain a healthy diet, get frequent exercise, and learn stress-reduction strategies. A sound body and mind serve as the cornerstone for long-term personal development.

5. **Collaboration and Networking:** - Establish a network of different people. Through networking, one can get new insights, collaborate with others, and find mentorship and learning opportunities.

6. **Embracing Challenges:** - View obstacles as chances for personal development. Go beyond your comfort zone, accept new responsibilities, and see obstacles as opportunities to grow resilient and acquire new abilities.

7. **Input and Ongoing Enhancement:** - Request input from coworkers, mentors, or peers. Giving constructive criticism promotes continuous personal growth by offering insightful information about areas that need work.

8. **Effective Time Management and Productivity:** - Make use

of efficient time management techniques. To increase productivity and make time for personal growth activities, organize your workload, establish priorities, and plan your time well.

1. The Adaptive Character of Ongoing Self-Improvement:

Maintaining progress requires understanding that constant self-improvement is an evolutionary process. As people advance on their path, their objectives, hopes, and sense of self may change. Accepting this evolutionary character means staying flexible, reevaluating objectives, and modifying tactics to conform to evolving situations and self-awareness.

Important Points Regarding the Evolutionary Character of Constant Self-Improvement:

1. **Reassessment of Goals:** - Review your professional and personal objectives on a regular basis. People change as they grow, and as a result, goals may need to be realigned to better reflect the values and priorities of the present.

2. **Adaptability in techniques:** - Show adaptability when modifying techniques. As circumstances change, what works at one point in the journey might need to be adjusted. Adaptability in methods guarantees ongoing applicability and efficiency.

3. **Incorporation of Lessons Learned:** - Incorporate what has been learned into continuing improvement. Gather insights from your experiences, triumphs, and failures to help you better understand yourself and guide your future development.

4. **Celebrating Milestones:** - Honor significant junctures along the journey. No matter how modest, celebrate your accomplishments since they add to the positive momentum of

ongoing self-improvement and serve as a source of motivation.

Result:

Constantly working on improving oneself is a transforming and evolutionary path that enables people to reach their greatest potential, deal with change, and have happy, satisfying lives. Underpinned by introspection, directed by core values, and reinforced by doable tactics, this dedication to continuous improvement is a powerful engine for individual development. People who accept challenges, develop a development mindset, and place a high value on their well-being set out on a journey that goes beyond achieving certain objectives and instead forges a lifetime course of self-discovery, resilience, and purpose.

Chapter 9: Integrating Emotional Mastery into Daily Life

9.1 Daily Habits for Sustaining High EI Levels

Success in both the personal and professional spheres is significantly influenced by emotional intelligence (EI), which is the capacity to identify, comprehend, and regulate one's own emotions in addition to skillfully navigating those of others. It takes regular work and the incorporation of daily routines that support emotional awareness, empathy, and productive interpersonal interactions to develop and maintain high emotional intelligence (EI) levels. In this investigation, we explore the routines that support emotional health, maintain high EI, and improve life pleasure in general.

1. **Morning Introspection and Mindfulness:**

Spend a little time being thoughtful at the start of the day. This can be as simple as taking a few minutes to center yourself and make good intentions for the day, or it might involve deep breathing exercises and meditation. **Consider Your Feelings:**

Think for a moment about how you are feeling. Recognize and accept any residual feelings from the previous day without passing judgment. Having self-awareness paves the way for purposeful emotional control throughout the day.

1. Journaling Frequently:

Keep a notebook to track your feelings and think back on them. Explain the circumstances that made you feel a certain way, evaluate your reactions, and think of different approaches to use in the future when faced with similar circumstances. Journaling develops emotional intelligence and self-awareness.

1. Mindful Practices for Communicating:

Make it a practice to actively listen to others when you interact. Ask clarifying questions, pay attention to the speaker's point of view, and refrain from interrupting. Building deeper interpersonal relationships and improving empathy are two benefits of active listening.

● Caring Reactions:

Prior to answering, especially in difficult circumstances, give your comments some thought. Emotionless reactions are detrimental to productive communication and conflict resolution. Instead, thoughtful responses are helpful. **4. Everyday Emotional Check-Ins:**

Allocate time during the day for quick emotional check-ins. To preserve emotional equilibrium, evaluate your emotional state, pinpoint any stressors or triggers, and make the required changes. Frequent emotional health check-ins improve self-control.

1. **Relaxation-Intentional Breaks:** Include deliberate pauses for rest and stress relief throughout the day. These little

excursions—whether they involve deep breathing techniques, a mindful moment, or a quick walk—help maintain emotional health and stave off burnout.

2. **Exercises in Gratitude:** Maintain a gratitude diary as a way to develop an attitude of thankfulness. Think of three things for which you are grateful each day, and then write them down. Practicing gratitude has been connected to higher levels of happiness and positive feelings in general.

3. **Activities to Foster Empathy:** Do random acts of kindness every day. These could be little acts of kindness like showing gratitude or lending a hand to a coworker. Kindness improves interpersonal connections and fosters the growth of empathy.

4. **Thoughtful Evening Ceremonies:** Review the day in brief before going to bed. Consider your relationships, emotional reactions, and any room for development. Engaging in reflective practice helps one become more self-aware and offers guidance for continued emotional development.

5. **Ongoing Education on Emotional Intelligence:** Set aside time to learn about emotional intelligence on a constant basis. Examine books, articles, or podcasts that discuss developing emotional intelligence. Continuous improvement is facilitated by remaining up to date on the most recent findings in emotional intelligence.

6. **Consistent Physical Activity:** Include physical activity on a regular basis in your schedule. Increased mental well-being, lowered stress levels, and happier moods have all been related to physical activity. You can have a favorable emotional influence from even a short workout.

7. **Conscious Eating: - Mindful Eating Practices:** Take a thoughtful approach to eating by giving each bite your whole attention. Eating mindfully helps you become more conscious of your body's signals and feelings toward food, which leads to

a more positive connection with eating.

8. **Evening Methods for Stress Reduction:**Create nighttime relaxation routines to help you wind down before going to bed. This could be reading, doing light stretching, or using relaxation techniques. Restful nighttime routines support emotional equilibrium and restful sleep.

9. **Practices for Social Connection:** Make meaningful social contacts a priority. Meaningful relationships with others, whether established in person, over the phone, or via video chat, promote emotional health and a sense of community.

10. **Establishing Limitations:** Define and uphold distinct boundaries between your personal and professional lives. Emotional resilience is facilitated by establishing reasonable expectations and striking a balance that permits personal time.

11. **Honor Triumphs:** Celebrate and recognize your accomplishments on a regular basis, no matter how small. Acknowledging achievements strengthens feelings of satisfaction and optimism.

Result:

Developing high emotional intelligence requires deliberate daily activities and is an ongoing process. These practices, which include self-awareness, self-reflection, empathic communication, and self-care, support long-term emotional health and productive interpersonal interactions. You may improve your emotional intelligence (EI) and the emotional atmosphere in both your personal and professional settings by adopting these regular routines. When these behaviors are combined, the result is a more emotionally intelligent, resilient, and contented person who can deal with life's challenges more readily.

9.2 Overcoming Common Challenges with Emotional Intelligence

In order to successfully navigate the complexities of interpersonal interactions and control one's emotions, emotional intelligence (EI) is a vital toolset. While having a high EI is advantageous, it's also critical to acknowledge and deal with the typical difficulties that people may face along the way. This investigation explores these issues and offers suggestions for using emotional intelligence to resolve them in a way that promotes development of the self, resilience, and stronger bonds between people.

1. **Difficulty: Impulsivity and Emotional Reactivity:** Impulsive emotional reactions are a typical problem, particularly in high-stress circumstances. Practicing self-regulation and increasing self-awareness to identify emotional triggers are key components of developing emotional intelligence. People can choose sensible reactions and improve outcomes by delaying gratification and averting confrontations.

2. **Difficulty Managing Criticism:** Emotionally charged criticism can make people defensive. People with emotional intelligence are more inclined to receive criticism with an open mind and a desire to learn. This entails distancing the criticism from oneself, appreciating the motivations behind it, and viewing it as a chance for development rather than a personal jab.

3. **Impaired Empathy:** Emotional intelligence is fundamentally based on empathy, yet some people find it difficult to relate to and comprehend the feelings of others. Active listening, adopting a perspective, and identifying the emotions that underlie both verbal and nonverbal signs are all necessary for

developing empathy. Building empathy improves communication between people and creates a cooperative and encouraging atmosphere.

4. **Difficulty: Poor Communication:**Conflicts and misunderstandings can result from poor communication. Effective communication is emphasized by emotional intelligence, which includes both active listening and thought-clearing expressiveness. Communication can be more empathic when people are aware of their emotions. This improves understanding between parties and lowers the possibility of misunderstandings.

5. Stress Management: One of the most important components of emotional intelligence is stress management. Relationships and decision-making may be hampered by high levels of stress. By implementing stress-reduction strategies like mindfulness, deep breathing, and time management, one can develop emotional intelligence. People who manage stress well are more emotionally resilient and have better decision-making skills.

6. **Difficulty:** Strong interpersonal skills are necessary for creating and maintaining meaningful connections. Comprehending social dynamics, engaging in skillful communication, and exhibiting empathy are all components of emotional intelligence. People with high EI actively cultivate relationships, which results in a pleasant and encouraging social network.

7. **Difficulty: Mental Tiredness: - Emotional Intelligence Remedy:** Emotional tiredness can result from constantly controlling emotions, whether they are personal or encountered in social situations. Acknowledging and meeting one's emotional needs is a necessary component of emotional intelligence. Emotional well-being and the avoidance of

burnout are enhanced by self-care, boundary-setting, and getting help when needed.

8. Fear of Vulnerability as a Challenge - **Emotional Intelligence Solution:** Vulnerability is encouraged as a strength rather than a weakness by those with emotional intelligence. Authentically admitting and expressing one's emotions is essential to overcoming the fear of vulnerability. Emotional intelligence and support are enhanced in relationships through the sharing of emotions, which also strengthens bonds of connection and trust.

9. **Difficulty: Dispelling Self-Limiting Thoughts: - Emotional Intelligence Solution:** Limiting thoughts can prevent one from growing both personally and professionally. Identifying and dispelling these myths is a key component of emotional intelligence. Reframing negative thinking, pursuing constructive criticism, and cultivating a growth mindset are strategies for breaking through self-limiting beliefs and promoting ongoing self-improvement.

10. **Difficulty: Juggling Emotional and Rational Thoughts: - Emotional Intelligence Solution:** Making decisions effectively requires balancing emotional and intellectual thought processes. Emotional intelligence is the ability to combine both analytical and affective thinking, taking into account the feelings involved in decisions while yet adhering to reason. This equilibrium guarantees knowledgeable and emotionally astute decision-making.

11. **Difficulty: Managing Uncertainty and Change: - EI Resolution:** Uncertainty and change can be emotionally taxing. Developing resilience and flexibility are components of emotional intelligence. Emotionally intelligent navigating of uncertainties involves cultivating a growth attitude, concentrating on controllable things, and seeing change as a

chance for learning.

12. **Difficulty: Identifying and Handling Bias: - Emotional Intelligence Solution:** Interactions and decision-making may be impacted by unconscious bias. Empathy to comprehend the viewpoints of others and self-awareness to identify biases are components of emotional intelligence. Fair and inclusive interactions and decision-making are facilitated by actively combating and minimizing bias.

13. **Difficulty: Juggling Personal and Professional Life: - Emotional Intelligence Solution:** Managing your personal and professional lives is a constant struggle. Establishing limits, arranging work in accordance with ideals, and using time management techniques are all components of emotional intelligence. Individuals can sustain their emotional well-being in both spheres of life by cultivating a healthy equilibrium.

14. **Difficulty: Gaining Patience: - Emotional Intelligence Solution:** Decision-making and communication can be hampered by impatience. Among the components of emotional intelligence are

gaining perspective and self-control can help with patience. Being aware that people connect at different speeds and with diverse viewpoints encourages interactions to be more patient and emotionally intelligent.

1. **Difficulty: Constructive Conflict Resolution: - Emotional Intelligence Solution:** Although conflict will inevitably arise, emotional intelligence offers strategies for amicable settlement. This entails figuring out win-win solutions, expressing emotions intelligently, and actively listening. Relationships are strengthened and conflict resolution is improved when conflicts are approached with empathy and a

collaborative perspective.

Result:

Overcoming typical obstacles with emotional intelligence is a life-changing process that calls for intentional practice, ongoing self-awareness, and a dedication to personal development. By utilizing emotional intelligence, people may help create emotionally intelligent and supportive settings in both the personal and professional domains in addition to efficiently navigating problems. A more purposeful and happy existence can result from identifying and resolving these issues using emotional intelligence, which also strengthens connections and resilience.

9.3 Mindfulness in Daily Activities

With roots in ancient contemplative traditions, mindfulness has become a potent practice in modern life, providing a means of achieving increased awareness, attention, and emotional well-being. Being totally present in the moment and interacting with one's sensations without passing judgment are the cornerstones of mindfulness. A revolutionary strategy for living more intentionally and cultivating a profound sense of inner calm is to incorporate mindfulness into everyday activities. This investigation explores the value of mindfulness in day-to-day activities, as well as its tenets and workable methods for incorporating mindfulness into daily existence.

1. Comprehending Mindfulness in Everyday Activities:

Developing present-moment awareness is the fundamental component of mindfulness. Those who practice mindfulness deliberately focus their attention on the present experience, which may be anything from a straightforward work to a discussion or a quiet period spent alone, instead of getting sucked into regrets from the past or anxieties about the future.

- **Observation Without Judgment:** The focus of mindfulness is on observing thoughts and feelings without passing judgment. Mindfulness fosters a compassionate relationship with the self by encouraging people to notice events with inquiry and acceptance, instead of categorizing them as good or negative.

2. **Mentality in Everyday Life:** Practicing mindfulness entails incorporating intentional presence into day-to-day activities. For example, while eating, walking, or working, the emphasis is on focusing entirely on the task at hand, without interruptions or mental clutter.

Recognition and Release: Accepting the situation as it is in the moment is encouraged by mindfulness. This entails adopting an accepting mentality that supports emotional resilience and letting go of resistance to situations, both good and bad.

- **Breath as an Anchor:**

- A fundamental anchor in mindfulness exercises is the breath. People may use their breath as a tool to build awareness and manage emotions, as well as to anchor oneself in the present moment.

3. Utilizing Mindfulness in Everyday Activities:

Savor every mouthful and concentrate on the whole dining experience to practice mindful eating. Take your time and thoroughly enjoy the flavors, textures, and experiences. Eating with awareness improves one's connection with food and makes meals more enjoyable.

Meditation while strolling:

Transform an ordinary stroll into a mindful stroll. Pay attention to every stride, the feeling of movement, and your connection to the earth. By converting a routine task into a thoughtful experience, this easy technique promotes serenity and presence.

- **Cognitive Task:**

Bring mindfulness to the office by giving each activity your whole attention. Instead of multitasking, focus only on each activity at hand, take brief mindfulness breaks to refresh and reset your mind throughout the day.

- **Mindful Communication:**

Engage in interactions with complete presence to practice mindful communication. React deliberately rather than impulsively, and listen intently to others without interrupting them. Intentional communication improves comprehension and fortifies relationships between people.

Cognitive Breathing:

Include conscious breathing in your regular activities. Take brief pauses to concentrate on your breathing, consciously inhaling and exhaling. In a variety of circumstances, mindful breathing acts as a transportable anchor, encouraging calmness and clarity.

● **Mindful Technology Use:**

Set deliberate limits to mindfully interact with technology. Avoid mindless scrolling, take pauses from displays, and exercise mindfulness when using electronics. Utilizing technology mindfully encourages a more deliberate and well-rounded approach to digital life.

● **Thoughtful Evening Meditation:**

Conclude the day with a thoughtful meditation. Examine the day's events objectively, noting both the difficulties and the happy times. This introspective activity helps one feel closure and gets the mind ready for sound sleep.

4. **Advantages of Mindfulness in Everyday Activities:**

Mindfulness is an effective method for reducing stress. People may end the cycle of tension and encourage a more serene, focused state of mind by practicing non-reactive awareness and present-moment awareness.

● **Improved Attention and Focus:** Frequent mindfulness exercises improve focus and sharpen attention. This increased focus translates into better productivity and the level of involvement with projects during everyday activities.

Control of Emotions: An emotional control framework is offered by mindfulness. People who are able to observe their emotions without reacting to them right away are better able to respond to events with more emotional intelligence, which in turn promotes emotional balance.

● **Enhanced Welfare:** Being mindful encourages a closer relationship with the present moment, which enhances general wellbeing. A happier and more positive perspective on life is a result of growing consciousness, accepting oneself, and adopting a nonjudgmental attitude toward situations.

5. **Developing an Intentional Way of Living: - Repetition is Crucial:** Being consistent is beneficial in the slow process of developing awareness. Over time, little, consistent actions incorporated into everyday life produce cumulative advantages.

● ** Begin with Daily Tasks:** Start by introducing awareness into routine, everyday tasks. As practicing mindfulness becomes second nature to daily duties, people can extend their practice to more intricate facets of life.

● **Communities of Mindfulness:** Taking part in guided sessions or being a part of mindfulness groups offers encouragement and support. Long-term mindfulness practice is aided by community resources and shared experiences.

A profound connection with the present moment is fostered by practicing mindfulness in daily activities, which is a transforming practice that encourages people to live more consciously. By accepting the tenets of mindfulness, implementing useful techniques into daily tasks, and realizing the numerous advantages

People may develop a mindful way of living that improves resilience, well-being, and a deep sense of inner peace. Being mindful broadens the definition of mindfulness from a practice to a way of life, providing a meaningful shift in viewpoint that enhances the fabric of everyday existence.

9.4 Managing Stress and Emotional Wellness

Stress has emerged as a common and often difficult feature to manage in the hectic and demanding world of contemporary living. Effective stress management, however, involves developing emotional wellbeing in order to preserve equilibrium and develop resilience, rather than just avoiding stressors. This study explores methods for reducing stress and promoting emotional health, shedding light on the connections between stress and emotions and suggesting doable solutions for resolving complicated situations in life with grace and resilience.

1. **Knowing How Stress and Emotional Well-Being Interact: - Reciprocal**

Relationship: Emotional well-being and stress are mutually correlated. Although stress may have a detrimental influence on one's emotional health, emotional wellbeing serves as a protective barrier against these harmful consequences. Developing resilience, cultivating an optimistic outlook, and identifying and skillfully regulating one's emotions are all components of emotional wellbeing.

2. **Stress Management Techniques: - Meditation and Mindfulness:** Practice mindfulness and meditation on a regular basis. These methods promote present-focused attention, enabling people to notice and deal with stresses in a composed and collected manner.

Active Exercise: Frequent exercise is an effective way to reduce stress. Exercise increases feelings of wellbeing and produces endorphins, the body's natural stress relievers. Exercise builds resilience in the body and the mind, whether it be via weight training, yoga, or aerobics.

- **Time Management Done Right:** To efficiently manage your time, prioritize your obligations and organize your chores. Divide more complex jobs into smaller, more doable stages so that everyday chores may be approached in a more organized and manageable manner.

- **Sleep Well Practices:** Make obtaining regular sleep schedules a priority for high-quality sleep. Emotional difficulties and stress might worsen when sleep deprived. Having a peaceful nighttime routine and a cozy sleeping space are important for general wellbeing.

Determining Limitations: Establish limits that are obvious to maintain a work-life balance. Stress may be caused by overcommitting and defining boundaries too loosely. People may live more harmoniously and stress-free by setting boundaries for their workload and making time for their hobbies.

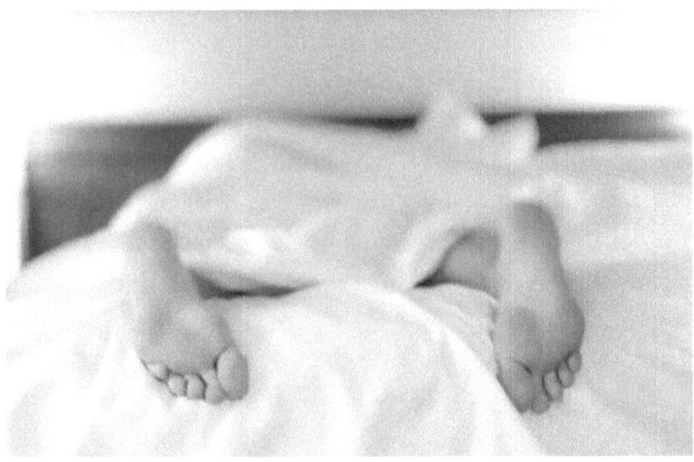

3. **Developing Emotional Well-Being: - Awareness of Oneself:** Self-awareness is the foundation of emotional wellbeing. Recognize and accept your feelings without passing judgment. Understanding the subtleties of emotions enables more thoughtful and purposeful reactions to challenges.

- **Effective Emotion Expression:** Create healthy channels for your emotions. This may include keeping a diary, creating art, or having frank discussions with reliable people. Stress levels might rise as a result of suppressing emotions.

- **Creating a Network of Support:** Create a solid support network by fostering deep connections. Making connections with loved ones, friends, or support groups offers a helpful network for exchanging stories, learning new viewpoints, and getting emotional support when things become hard.

- **Physical-Mind Techniques:** Examine mind-body techniques including tai chi, yoga, and deep breathing exercises. These activities provide a comprehensive approach to stress management by improving emotional control, resilience, and physical well-being.

- **Cognitive Restructuring:** Using cognitive restructuring, question and reframe unfavorable thinking processes. Recognize and swap out unreasonable or harmful ideas with more sensible and positive ones. Stress reduction and enhanced emotional well-being are two benefits of this cognitive technique.

4. **Combining Emotional Wellbeing with Stress Management: - Whole Lifestyle Approach:** Understand the connections between stress reduction and emotional well-being as components of a comprehensive way of living. Taking an integrated approach means treating mental, emotional, and physical health at the same time.

• **Consistent Visits:** Make sure to regularly assess your mental health as well as your stress levels. Identifying stresses, thinking back on feelings, and evaluating general wellbeing all help to reveal areas that could need correction or attention. **Conscientious Decision-Making:** Make thoughtful decisions by weighing the stress and emotional effects of your options. By enabling people to make choices that are consistent with their beliefs, mindfulness helps people avoid stressful situations and foster emotional congruence.

• **Developing Good Habits:** Incorporate healthy routines that support emotional and stress relief into your everyday existence. This might include making time for mindfulness exercises, taking up hobbies, and giving pleasure and fulfillment-bringing pursuits top priority.

5. **Expert Guidance and Materials: - Medical Interventions:** Seek expert assistance via therapeutic treatments as necessary. Counseling, cognitive-behavioral therapy (CBT), and other therapeutic approaches may provide useful resources for stress management and enhancing emotional well-being.

• **Reference Materials:** Get instructional materials about emotional health and stress reduction. Online tools, seminars, books, and articles all provide insightful information and useful tactics for preserving emotional equilibrium and fostering resilience.

6. **Building Resilience in the Face of Challenges:** - **Adaptive Coping Strategies:** Learn how to deal with obstacles by developing flexible coping mechanisms. This entails adopting a growth mindset, taking lessons from failures, and seeing obstacles as chances for emotional and personal development.

● **Adaptability and Flexibility:** Develop these qualities to better handle change. The capacity to face uncertainty with optimism and the readiness to modify objectives and standards when necessary are traits of resilience.

A dedication to comprehensive well-being and deliberate effort are necessary for the continuous and interwoven journey that is stress management and emotional health cultivation. People may overcome obstacles in life with perseverance and strength by adopting a healthy lifestyle, developing self-awareness, and using useful techniques.

Understanding how stress and emotions interact dynamically enables people to proactively control both, leading to a happier and more satisfying existence. In the end, pursuing emotional well-being turns into a transforming process that helps people adopt a resilient and well-rounded perspective on the challenges of everyday life.

9.5 Celebrating Successes and Continued Growth

In addition to serving as a fleeting acknowledgement of accomplishments, celebrating victories is essential for maintaining a good outlook and promoting ongoing personal and professional development. This investigation explores the value of acknowledging accomplishments, the psychological advantages it provides, and methods for building a culture of acknowledgment that encourages people to keep moving ahead on their path of self-improvement.

1. Comprehending the Significance of Festivity:

Rejoicing in accomplishments has a significant psychological impact on people. It gives one a feeling of achievement, raises one's self-esteem, and supports constructive conduct. No matter how large or tiny, acknowledging accomplishments helps one stay happy and motivated to work toward bigger objectives.

- **Building Inspiration:**

Joy serves as a strong incentive. A positive reinforcement loop is created when people feel the happiness and acknowledgement that come with achievement, which motivates them to set and achieve new objectives with zeal and tenacity.

2. The Significance of Acknowledgment in Ongoing Development:

Acknowledgment affirms the efforts and diligence devoted to accomplishing an objective. It conveys the perception that one's efforts are appreciated, which strengthens one's sense of purpose and the notion that persistent work produces fruitful results.

- **Developing Self-Belief:**

Celebrating accomplishments boosts self-assurance. Taking on more responsibility and seeking new challenges both need confidence. People are inspired to push themselves and seize fresh chances by the confidence that comes from prior accomplishments.

- **Promoting the Take-Risk:**

Acknowledging successes promotes a risk-taking attitude. People are more willing to leave their comfort zones, investigate novel ideas, and take on challenges that advance their professional and personal development when they feel that their efforts are valued and encouraged.

3. Tips for Successful Celebration:

Honor both minor and major accomplishments. Acknowledging little victories makes the environment happier and inspires people to keep going on their development path.

- **Personalized Recognition:** Adapt recognition to the preferences of certain persons. While some people may value appreciation in public, others would prefer recognition that is given in private. Making celebrations unique guarantees that people are noticed and valued in a manner that speaks to them.

- **Team Celebrations:** Expand the festivities to include the whole team. Acknowledging group accomplishments strengthens the bond between participants and the notion that success requires cooperation. Celebrations held as a team help to foster a happy and encouraging work environment.

Regular Check-Ins: Include contemplation and celebration periods at regular intervals. Regular evaluations of accomplishments, significant events, and advancements foster a culture that values ongoing development and provides chances for acknowledgment.

- **Symbolic gestures:** Honor accomplishments using symbolic gestures. These might be honors, diplomas, or sentimental items that people can proudly exhibit. Symbolic acknowledgment creates a strong emotional bond and acts as a concrete reminder of accomplishments.

4. Create a Culture of Continuous Improvement:
Promote introspection about accomplishments. Examining

the factors that led to success provides insightful information for next projects. A growth mentality and a focus on ongoing progress are enhanced by learning from achievements.

Assigning Novel Tasks: Celebrate accomplishments by posing fresh difficulties. The drive to pursue new objectives might be directed toward accomplishments. Establishing and fulfilling more difficult goals promotes a culture of continuous improvement.

- **Promoting mentoring:** Encourage mentoring among community members. Well-known people may act as mentors, imparting their knowledge and perspectives to others. Mentoring promotes knowledge and skill transfer and fosters a collaborative learning environment.

- **Opportunities for Professional growth:** Build your professional growth on your accomplishments. Acknowledgments for accomplishments may lead to additional chances for leadership, skill development, or training, all of which can advance an individual's development.

5. Overcoming Difficulties and Gaining Knowledge from Them: Acknowledge setbacks as essential components of the learning process. Honoring accomplishments is about being resilient in the face of difficulty, not about avoiding obstacles. Recognize failures, draw lessons from them, and see them as chances for further development.

- **Adapting and Iterating:** Adopt an iterative and adaptive mentality. Honoring achievements does not suggest a static condition but rather a continuous process of modification and advancement. It is important to support individuals and groups in building on their achievements and looking for methods to improve procedures and results.

Result:

A transforming habit, celebrating triumphs goes beyond just recognizing them when they are accomplished. It establishes a constructive cycle of inspiration, self-assurance, and ongoing development. People and organizations may create an atmosphere that supports both professional and personal development by accepting setbacks as chances for progress, recognizing the psychological effects of acknowledgment, and encouraging a culture of celebration.

Effective celebrations enable people to contribute to a culture of achievement and development that benefits the community as a whole, while also inspiring them to achieve new heights. Acknowledging successes turns into more than simply a brief stop for celebration—rather, it serves as a spark for continued momentum and a joint effort to continuously improve.

Conclusion

This adventure into the realms of emotional intelligence has been a voyage of self-discovery, development, and connectivity in the fabric of emotions that constitute the human experience. This inquiry comes to an end, but emotional intelligence continues to resonate as the unifying theme that runs through all the many chapters of our life.

Each chapter has been a brushstroke on the canvas of emotional mastery, covering everything from techniques for emotion management to the subtleties of sympathetic understanding. We've explored the boundaries of motivation, gone down to the depths of resilience, and seen firsthand how empathy can change both our personal and professional relationships. We have accepted change, dismantled self-limiting beliefs, and followed the never-ending path of self-improvement through the prism of emotional intelligence.

Emotional intelligence has a bright future, but it also comes with responsibilities. The ethical integration of emotional intelligence in robotics and artificial intelligence becomes a light pointing the way toward a future that is compassionate and well-balanced as technology becomes more and more integrated with our knowledge of emotions. The way that cultural standards are changing as a result of inclusion and empathy serves as a constant reminder of our common humanity and the possibility of future improvement.

The significance of global emotional intelligence as a uniting factor in our linked world is shown in the last threads of the tapestry. Fostering empathy across national boundaries, comprehending varied viewpoints, and appreciating the emotional complexity of international societies become more than simply goals; they are necessities for a peaceful and sustainable future.

Let's apply the teachings of emotional intelligence to our everyday lives as we wrap up this chapter. Let us be the designers of understanding, the builders of resilience, and the architects of empathy.

Let emotional intelligence be the lighthouse that guides our relationships in our families, businesses, and communities, transforming difficult situations into chances for connection.

I hope that the knowledge presented in these pages strikes a chord in your souls and causes a beneficial chain reaction. Allow emotional intelligence to serve as your compass as you navigate the ups and downs of life, serving as a constant reminder that our common humanity is embodied in the enormous array of emotions.

As the last words are spoken, keep in mind that developing emotional intelligence is a lifelong journey rather than a destination. This journey invites you to appreciate the beauty of emotions, form meaningful connections with others, and, in the process, create a world where empathy, understanding, and emotional intelligence are the cornerstones of our shared story.

May your heart play the emotional intelligence melody in the symphony of human connection, bringing harmony and enrichment to your life and the lives of others around you.

Don't miss out!

Visit the website below and you can sign up to receive emails whenever Dr M.k.Brown publishes a new book. There's no charge and no obligation.

https://books2read.com/r/B-A-BFADB-IIKUC

BOOKS 2 READ

Connecting independent readers to independent writers.